The 8th Chakra

Hay House Titles of Related Interest

Chakra Clearing: *Awakening Your Spiritual Power to Know and Heal* (book-with-CD), by Doreen Virtue, Ph.D.

Four Paths of Personal Power: *How to Heal Your Past and Create a Positive Future,* by Denise Linn

The Divine Matrix: *The Pure Space Where All Things Begin,* by Gregg Braden

Archangels & Ascended Masters: *A Guide to Working and Healing with Divinities and Deities,* by Doreen Virtue, Ph.D.

Remembering the Future: *The Path to Recovering Intuition,* by Colette Baron-Reid

Quantum Success: *The Astounding Science of Wealth and Happiness,* by Sandra Anne Taylor

Soul Lessons and Soul Purpose: *A Channeled Guide to Why You Are Here,* by Sonia Choquette

All of the above are available at your local bookstore, or may be ordered by visiting:

Hay House USA: **www.hayhouse.com**®
Hay House Australia: **www.hayhouse.com.au**
Hay House UK: **www.hayhouse.co.uk**
Hay House India: **www.hayhouse.co.in**

The 8th Chakra

What It Is and How It Can Transform Your Life

Jude Currivan, Ph.D.

HAY HOUSE, INC.
Carlsbad, California • New York City
London • Sydney • New Delhi

Library of Congress Control Number: 2006926569

ISBN 13: 978-1-4019-1695-4

1st edition, May 2007
2nd edition, June 2008

Printed in the United States of America

From the Editor: To our American readers,
please note that we have maintained the British style of
spelling, grammar, punctuation, and syntax of the original text
in order to preserve the editorial intent of the author
(who hails from the United Kingdom).

The Native American spiritual traditions recognize that we are all related – people, animals, trees and all the realms of the living Earth and the wider Cosmos. The 8th Chakra is dedicated with the unconditional love of the universal heart to all our relations.

CONTENTS

Acknowledgements

My darling mother used to say with a smile that I'd speak with anyone.

Since the age of four I've spoken with and, more importantly, learned from not only the people I've loved, laughed, cried and argued with, but also animals, nature spirits, Devas, Angels, ghosts, Ascended Masters, ancient gods and cosmic guides.

I honour them all as fellow travellers and I love and thank them for whatever reason and in whatever way we have journeyed together, whether for a moment, a season or an eternity.

In writing *The 8th Chakra*, my love and gratitude are given especially to the following beings:

Michelle Pilley of Hay House, whose wisdom, encouragement and trust are a priceless gift to me.

My editor, Lizzie Hutchins, whose extraordinary insight and expertise brought the book to life.

My dear friend Jeannie Kar, a true soular hero.

My beloved husband, Tony, for whose ever-present love and support my words can never be enough.

And my mentor and guide, Thoth, who has been with me from the beginning of everything.

Introduction

As I begin to write, today is 23rd December. On this winter solstice dawn, the Sun has once more commenced its yearly spiral from darkness to light. Since ancient times, this day has traditionally welcomed the birth of the archetypal solar hero, who has been known by many names and whose outer quest and inner journey to wholeness have been depicted in many mythic sagas and myriad spiritual teachings.

The solar hero was never meant to be worshipped; rather, he was meant to be emulated. For each and every one of us has this divine potential within us. Yet for 2,000 years, the voice of the greatest of solar heroes has gone unheeded. Jesus said, in John 14:12, 'As I do these things, so shall ye do them, and greater.'

We are the ones he spoke of. But over the last two millennia, first institutionalized religion sought to convince us of our unworthiness and then science sought to persuade us that only the material world was 'real'.

However, a new vision of the Cosmos is now emerging, one which is reconciling science and spiritual wisdom in a more profound and personally empowering way than ever before. It is offering us not only answers to the questions of *how* the Cosmos is as it is, but also the chance to understand *why* it is as it is.

This new awareness has radical implications for each and every one of us. For it reveals a wholly interconnected, conscious and holographic universe, a Cosmos where consciousness is primary – and where we are therefore both creation and co-creator.

Our highest purpose in being here at this momentous time is to remember this, and in doing so to re-member who we *really* are. We are now able to access newly available cosmic energies that transcend our personal sense of self. They liberate our perception, enabling us to heal and release old patterns and limitations. And, as we free ourselves, we are empowered to fully embody the higher purpose of our soul and to consciously co-create the emergence of a new cosmic age – an age in which we all have the potential to real-ize that we are solar – or soular – heroes.

The 8th Chakra

The earliest spiritual traditions perceived ego consciousness as mediated through seven energetic vortices that they called 'chakras'. In recent years, this ancient wisdom has become much more widely known and accepted.

Collectively, however, we know at a deep level that our personal energy field of seven chakras is incomplete. This can be shown by the cosmic resonance embodied in the 13 notes of the complete chromatic musical scale and the eight notes of its diatonic sub-scale. Singing the first seven notes of the diatonic scale – doh, ray, me, fa, soh, la, te – leaves us feeling that something is missing.

And so it is. It is the eighth note that completes the octave and the 8th chakra that completes the octave of our personality-based consciousness. The 8th chakra is also the energetic portal to our higher awareness, guidance and soul-level purpose.

Unity Awareness

The 8th chakra is the first transpersonal chakra of our unity awareness. Unity awareness is consciousness of the greater whole of which we are all part and which we are now able to embody in human form. Accessing such expanded awareness enables us to transcend the limitations of our human perception and re-member that we are not alone but ultimately are all-one. We are thus empowered to real-ize the holographic nature of the Cosmos, the One expressed through the almost infinite diversity of the many.

For millennia we have experienced the polarities of light and shadow in all their rich expression. Now is the time for us to take conscious responsibility for our destiny and embody the transpersonal awareness that offers us a way home to the unity that lies beyond all polarities. This is the destination of the soular hero.

This book shares how to access these transpersonal energies to empower greater perception and undertake heart-centered healing at a soul level. It shows how we can experience all that we really are through our minds, emotions and bodies and how we can re-establish profound relationships with ourselves, our human family, Gaia (the living Earth), and the wider Cosmos.

Every one of us walks a unique path to an ultimate destination shared by us all. *The 8th Chakra* is a way-shower for the soular hero in all of us, enabling each of us to choose our own way forward.

Re-member

Every journey begins with a first step, which we often only perceive in hindsight. The first step of my own journey to the 8th chakra started, as it did for us all, aeons ago. But I first became aware of the path when, literally out of the blue, I received a psychic message in early May 1998. Whilst I have received such higher guidance since early childhood, this message was particularly clear. It opened up a path that became the most challenging I have ever walked, for it asked me to re-member who I *really* am – not just the Jude I thought I knew, but all the aspects of my dis-membered psyche.

I began to re-member not only my personality-based awareness but higher levels of archetypal and cosmic consciousness as I journeyed from being all-one to *knowing* that we are all-one. That journey took me around the world and is related in my forthcoming book *The 13th Step*. It opened me to the realities of the 8th chakra and the higher perception that is our individual and collective heritage and cosmic destiny. It is this awareness that is shared in this book.

Why Now?

The holographic universe is innately interconnected, conscious and purposeful. There are *no* accidents!

Individually and collectively, we have trodden an age-old journey to this moment in time. It has been a journey during which, as spiritual beings undertaking a physical experience, we have explored *all* that it means to be human.

Or have we?

Prophecies ranging from those of the ancient Maya to those of contemporary mystics and the elders of the primary people who still walk the Earth state that this is a time of transformation. The Mayan calendar ends at the December solstice of 2012, which they perceived as being the culmination of myriad cycles of consciousness and presaging a Shift in collective awareness.

All that I have understood on my own journey to this point is that this Shift is the precursor to our consciously embodying our spiritual wholeness in our experience of being human.

The living Earth has been our cradle and she remains our home. But it's now time for us to grow up.

HoME-coming

The 8th Chakra is structured in three parts, reflecting the three-in-one nature of all initiatory experiences. Also, since the inner journey to spiritual wholeness has traditionally been embodied in 12 around 1, culminating in the transformative 13th, *The 8th Chakra* has 13 chapters. The path is as follows:

Part I, encompassing the first four chapters, shares, in an accessible way, how leading-edge science is reconciling with spiritual tradition to develop a universal model of cosmic consciousness. It also explains what this means for each and every one of us.

Part II, Chapters 5 to 8, explores who we *really* are. It reveals that we are microcosms within a vast holographic Cosmos and shows how we can begin to embody cosmic harmony.

Part III, Chapters 9 to 13, describes, in an empowering and practical way, the steps to our self-realization – how we may embody the magnificent wholeness of our spiritual nature and express it in every aspect of our lives.

The 8th Chakra is ultimately a call for us to re-member who we really are. In choosing to be here at this momentous time in the story of humanity, we have all given ourselves the opportunity to fulfil our highest soul purpose: to come HoME by co-creating Heaven on Mother Earth.

We'll now set the context of our journey by taking a brief tour of the holographic universe.

PART I

Understand

❖❖❖❖

CHAPTER 1

The Cosmic Hologram

Astronomers now understand that at the very beginning of space and time the universe was set up in an incredibly ordered way which enabled the 'arrow' of time to begin its flight. They also now know that the initial conditions from which the universe was born were exquisitely fine-tuned, thereby enabling the evolution of biological life. And they are now aware that many dimensions are required to satisfy the natural laws that underlie the physical world. Perhaps most profoundly, they are coming to entertain the view that the universe and all that it contains may be the projection of a cosmic hologram.

Scientists undertaking research into a variety of complex systems – from biological organisms to economics, weather patterns to human conflicts – are also becoming aware of the same underlying holographic principle.

Understanding the nature of the cosmic hologram is now appearing to be key to our understanding the universe. But what is a hologram and how is it created?

The Hologram

A hologram is produced when a single beam of coherent light, such as that of a laser, is split into two. One beam is bounced off an object and the second beam is aligned to interfere with the reflected light of the first. The resulting wave pattern is then recorded on film. When light is subsequently shone through the two-dimensional film, a three-dimensional image of the object – or hologram – is then projected.

Holograms are now mundanely seen on credit cards, which reveal a small holographic image that comes to life when aligned with light.

One of the most significant aspects of the holographic principle is that the entirety of the whole object is re-created in every part of its three-dimensional image. So, if a holographic projection is subdivided into millions of pieces, every single piece will incorporate a tiny and complete representation of the whole.

The mathematics that describes the hologram enables *any* physical pattern to be transformed into waveforms and converted back to its original shape. Such holographic 'transforms' are also related to the analytical tools that have recently been developed to describe complex systems both natural and man-made. These have revealed underlying geometric patterns called 'fractals'. Their interrelationships are the innate reality from which the diverse world of form is manifested. Their harmonic nature is seen both in their self-similarity, where each part is similar to the whole, and their scale-invariance, whereby their inherent patterns remain unchanged whether scaled up or down in size.

Scientifically, the description of the Cosmos in holographic terms is relatively new, yet the idea is millennia old. The teaching ascribed to the archetypal wisdom-bringer known as Thoth to the ancient Egyptians, 'As above, so below', describes the One as manifest in the diversity of the many and the microcosm as embodying the totality of the macrocosm. This perfectly reflects the reality of the hologram.

Cosmic Mind

Science is also beginning to rediscover the ancient insights that viewed the manifest universe as an all-pervasive cosmic mind. In this world-view, consciousness is not only present at all scales of existence, it *is* existence itself. It both transcends and pervades the entirety of space and time.

Hitherto, science has sought to understand *how* the universe is as it is, leaving the question of *why* it is as it is to philosophers. But now the necessary inclusion of consciousness in the emerging world-view no longer allows the question of 'why' to be excluded from the exploration of the greater realities of the Cosmos.

My book *The Wave* explores how leading-edge science and the latest research into consciousness are reconciling science and Spirit. In *The 8th Chakra*, we'll undertake our journey to understand who we really are from the perspective that consciousness *is* primary and does indeed cause the myriad effects that we call the physical world.

All the energies and matter that comprise the physical world have been present from its very beginning and will be until its end. Their vast diversity of forms arises from underlying patterns that are innately harmonious. And throughout Nature consciousness continually co-creates through the alchemical transformations we call 'life'.

Consciousness expresses itself as energy, which manifests as waves. The cosmic hologram of the physical world is then continually co-created from their interference patterns.

To understand how the universe is exquisitely set up to enable the exploration of consciousness, we now need to delve into its fundamental energetic principles.

And to do that we need to journey back 13.7 billion years to its birth.

Light and Sound

The big bang theory which cosmologists use to describe the creation of the physical world shows that its birth was neither big nor a bang.

From an almost unimaginably minute genesis, the universe inflated as an impeccably ordered wave of space and time – a cosmic out-breath rather than an explosion.

The Vedic tradition of ancient India, the Taoists of China and the writers of the Bible all perceived that the universe was sung into being by primal sound – the Word of creation. In India, the physical manifestation of this cosmic vibration is the *Aum*. Similarly in ancient China, the foundation tone of imperial music was the *huang chung*, the 'yellow bell' deemed to be the audible equivalent of the divine note.

The ancients also understood the inherent role of light – the visible part of the spectrum of electromagnetic energies – in the manifestation of physical form. Perhaps this is best depicted in the biblical 'Let there be Light'. In a profound way, these metaphysical depictions of the ancients presage today's cosmological insights.

Space and Time

In common parlance, space and time are separate, but in reality they are not. As our universe expands, its fabric is woven together by (and at the speed of) light into the four-dimensional entity cosmologists call 'spacetime'.

Cosmologists now know that at the beginning of the universe spacetime was in an incredibly ordered state. This is crucial because in any system, order will always tend towards disorder – as any of you with children will know. So the initial order of spacetime could only evolve one way – to greater overall disorder. It is this, cosmologists believe, which enabled the direction of universal time, which we call its 'arrow', to be embodied.

But the level of disorder, or 'entropy', of a system is also a measure of the amount of information held within it. This is because the level of disorder is equivalent to the number of available states its fundamental elements can embody. The greater the number of states, the greater the level of information within them. So, since the birth of the universe, nearly 14 billion years ago, as its overall level of disorder has inexorably increased, the physical world has been enabled to embody ever more information and awareness.

Real-ativity

Spacetime is not, however, an absolute and passive backdrop to the universe. It is relative to the position of an observer and is also dynamic with regard to that observer's movement.

Observers in relative motion to each other will measure time differently, and these differences are not merely personal perceptions but are the relativity – or real-ativity – of the way the physical world actually is. For example, let's imagine two observers on a space station synchronizing their watches. One then remains on the station whilst the other joins the crew of a spaceship able to travel at 87 per cent of the speed of light. As the spaceship subsequently reaches its maximum speed, whilst the observer on board measures his own time as 'normal', he would, if he were able to, discern that time for his friend left at the station is passing twice as fast. Conversely, for the observer at the station, his own time is passing normally, whilst he observes that time on the spaceship is running at half the 'normal' speed.

However, unlike the movement of everything else in the universe, from snails to stars, the speed of light is *always* measured as being constant, no matter how fast an observer approaches or moves away it. This is because as the speed of an observer – or indeed any physical object – increases, time *itself* progressively slows down in perfect correspondence so that the speed of light is always measured as being the same. Yet to each observer, the measurement of their own time appears normal. This perception of normality is crucial, because it means that the laws of physics themselves are identical to all observers undergoing constant-velocity motion, regardless of their vantage point in the universe.

The speed of light, known as 'c' (from the Latin *celeritas*, meaning 'rapid'), is the fastest speed possible within spacetime and is thus the upper limit of the transmission of all information within the physical world. The combined attributes of this inherent limitation and the universal arrow of time embed the principle of causality within the very nature of spacetime.

This fundamental principle enables the universe to unfold and evolve. It also allows the level of consciousness associated with the ego-self – for not only humans but all self-aware life forms – to experience the implications of making choices through the creative processes of cause and effect. In this way we accrue learning and understanding.

Universal Forces

The Taoist philosophers of ancient China described the origin of the physical world as being the sundering of unity into the universal polarities of yang and yin. Whilst now four apparently distinct forces have been recognized as regulating matter and energy, cosmologists also believe that at the inception of the universe they were essentially one.

The first of the four universal forces is electromagnetism. This is intrinsic to the holographic principle and the mediation of consciousness into physical expression.

Two other forces only operate at the tiny scale of the atom – the so-called strong nuclear force which binds the nuclei of atoms together and the weak nuclear force which accounts for phenomena such as radioactive decay.

The fourth force is gravity, whose power to attract increases in relation to the masses of objects. It is thus only discernible in the large-scale interaction of matter.

The relative strengths of these four forces and the scales over which they operate are wonderfully balanced to facilitate the evolution of complexity. If gravity were only marginally stronger or if the electrical or nuclear forces were slightly weaker, stars would not shine and biological life would not be possible.

Over the last century, scientists have sought not only to understand each of these forces but also to bring them all into a unified vision of Nature. But it is only recently that cosmologists have been able to formulate a view of the universe that holds the potential for such unification. To do so, they have needed to perceive Nature in the same way as the philosophers of the ancient world.

The Cosmic Symphony

The ancient sages intuitively understood the physical world as being essentially harmonic and described it in musical terms.

In modern times, Einstein offered us the first clue that the ancients were correct when he revealed that all matter was essentially standing waves of energy conjoined by the speed of light. He described this in his famous equation $E=mc^2$, showing that the energy of an object, E, is equal to the product of its mass, m, and the speed of light, c, multiplied by itself.

Matter and energy were once considered to be made up of point-like 'particles'. During the last decade, however, this understanding has been replaced by the concept that all energy and matter is fundamentally made up of ultra-minute waveforms called 'strings'. The theory runs that the oscillatory patterns and resonance of these strings form the fundamental 'notes' of the cosmic symphony that is the universe.

An intrinsic requirement of this developing theory is that strings vibrate not in our familiar four-dimensional spacetime (three dimensions of space and one of time), but in 11 dimensions. This acknowledgement of higher dimensions is a leap forward in our understanding of supra-physical realities. But it is further fundamental elements of string theory that may be the key to the most profound revelation yet of our understanding of the Cosmos. These are multi-dimensional objects called 'branes'. They theoretically form the framework within which strings oscillate and to which they are energetically connected. Astoundingly, cosmologists are also beginning to suspect that branes may form the boundary of spacetime and are the means by which the entire physical world is holographically projected.

Quantum Notes

Of crucial significance has been the further realization that the vibrations of these fundamental entities of Nature are not continuous, but change their form in discrete steps, with a minimum packet or 'quantum' of energy associated with each frequency. Scientists describe such 'quanta' as existing in 'quantum states' and the spontaneous shift from one state to another as a 'quantum jump'. Just as there are no intermediate stages between one musical note and another, so there are none between one quantum state and another.

Such quantization is critical for the holographic principle to operate, because whole quanta of energies are required to enable the phenomena of coherence and resonance – that is, physical manifestation – to occur. The same is true for the whole notes that manifest musical harmony.

Nonlocality

Until observed the quantum building blocks of the entire universe exist only as probabilities. But experiments show that when we observe a quantum entity – or, significantly, have the intention to do so – it becomes coherent and is realized or, as quantum physicists say, 'actualized'.

Such evidence reveals that we can no longer consider an observer and what is observed as separate. And whilst for many years science has insisted that such quantum effects are limited to the minute world of fundamental particles, this is increasingly being shown not to be the case.

This recognition is profoundly associated with one of the most intriguing aspects of quantum behaviour. Termed 'nonlocality', it is the experimentally proven fact that quanta can be instantaneously connected and are effectively a single entity – even if separated by the entire universe.

Researchers investigating phenomena such as telepathy and remote viewing have revealed that the human mind also acts nonlocally. In such cases we can perceive events and obtain information beyond the limitations of our physical senses. Communication can transcend spacetime and consequentially does not rely on any signal or influence travelling *within* the universe.

Essentially what this means is that within the physical world, influence is mediated by the speed of light. Therefore causality and the arrow of time are preserved. Yet at nonlocal levels of perception, which include higher levels of individual and collective consciousness, awareness is not bound by the confines of space and time.

The Universal DVD

We now need to go even further beyond the limitations of our linear perception of time and begin to attune to the deeper nature of the Cosmos.

Within spacetime, the perception that space exists in its entirety is familiar to us. But as space and time form a single entity, the entirety of time also exists all at once. So, as Einstein pointed out, the perception of the flow of time by our conscious mind is, in essence, a mental construction.

In the symmetry of the universe, no vantage point in space or time is more valid than any other – reality encompasses all such 'nows' without distinction between past, present and future. It is only in our mental freeze-frame that a sequence of events seems to evolve as a continuous story. Rather like a DVD – which also works on holographic principles – every moment of 'now' is a still frame which, when run together in sequence with all the others, creates a continuous story and enables a coherent experience to unfold.

However, as with a story captured on DVD, the perception of change does embody a direction in time. And the future is inherently different from the past. As we shall see, whilst the underlying fabric of time is ever present, the information relating to events is progressively imprinted as the story unfolds.

The deep mystery of time is one to which we shall return in Chapter 4, as it has profound consequences for our understanding of free will and destiny.

Archetypal Patterns

Let's now turn – perhaps with a sigh of relief – to aspects of the world that are more familiar parts of our everyday experience.

In ancient times, geometers intuitively discerned that archetypal patterns and harmony were the underlying templates for the diversity we see in Nature. The limited analytical tools at their disposal meant, however, that they were unable to probe deeply into natural phenomena, such as weather patterns, which are complex or exhibit chaotic behaviour. However, in the 1960s, with the advent of computers, a greater understanding of such complex systems became possible.

Since then, researchers have scrutinized a vast range of data concerning a variety of systems exhibiting fluctuations and irregularities, whether occurring in space or time. What they have discovered is a holographic revelation of self-similar fractal patterns repeating at ever-larger and smaller scales. From earthquakes to economics, from the incidence of conflicts to the shapes of coastlines, from biological ecosystems to the worldwide web, the harmonic signature of the holographic principle has been revealed.

Beneath apparent chaos, there is order.

Power Laws

As an example, before this 'complexity theory' was developed, most researchers sought to understand and predict the occurrence of earthquakes using statistical methods. They attempted to determine their frequency and scale according to the premise that a 'typical' earthquake could be so described. But it can't.

What seismologists have found instead is that over an enormously wide range, the frequencies of earthquakes correspond in a direct way with the energy they release – an earthquake twice as powerful is four times less likely to occur.

Where, as in the case of earthquakes, the continuing doubling of the frequency of one factor (e.g., the energy released) elicits a constant response in the frequency of another factor (e.g., the rate of occurrence), the harmonic nature of the phenomenon and the resonance underlying its entire manifestation are revealed. Such a relationship is known as a 'power law'.

The inherent simplicity of holographic power laws underlies the complexity of the phenomena they describe. Any system which obeys a power law is scale-invariant, self-similar and based on a fractal pattern – and as such the term 'typical' just doesn't apply.

Harmonic Cycles

These complex systems all exhibit what is called 'non-linear behaviour'. In other words, a small cause can set off a large effect, or vice versa. Such effects can then become the causes of further larger or smaller effects, which may in turn feed back to the initiating cause, creating harmonic cycles of behaviour.

Such systems have been revealed as innately holographic in nature. For when the variables describing their behaviour have been traced mathematically, they have been discovered to take the shapes of what are known as 'attractors'. Such attractors are essentially the energetic templates from which such systems manifest.

To the great surprise of scientists, it appears that there are only three types of attractor, each of which is generic to specific phenomena. The attractors that underlie many complex systems are, perhaps not surprisingly, called 'strange'. And it is these that are embedded within all the complex phenomena mentioned above.

Critical States

Whilst complexity theory can explain unpredictability, by itself it isn't enough to explain major shifts or upheavals. For this we need to develop a deeper understanding of systems that are not in balance, especially those that are poised on the knife-edge between order and chaos.

Such non-linear systems, where a tiny event can trigger either a small dislocation or a catastrophic upheaval, are inherently unstable and described as being 'in a critical state'. They are found across a huge range of phenomena and their mathematical signature has been discerned in events as apparently diverse as the contagion of epidemics, the collapse of ecosystems, stock-market crashes and the spread of forest fires.

Increasingly it is being recognized that interconnecting networks of many types have a tendency to naturally organize themselves in such states when open to the flow of energy. How they behave appears to be solely due to the basic relational issue of how easy it is for an ordering or disordering influence at one point in the system to bring order or disorder to another point nearby. In addition, *only* the physical dimensions of the elements of the system and their basic geometric shape matter in effecting this influence and thus the behaviour of the system – nothing else.

Such amazing universality tells us that if the characteristics of one example in a universal class of phenomena are understood, then all other members of that class are understood too.

It also reveals that if the fundamental factors of elemental size and shape are understood, then the diversity of the system can be modelled without recourse to the myriad of other details it exhibits.

Again, the more deeply we peer beneath the diversity of manifestation, the more we discover harmony and underlying order – the cosmic hologram of consciousness at work.

Feedback

Where an influence generated by one element in a system on another results in a reverse influence, the system is said to exhibit 'feedback'. When the processes of feedback are irreversible, what happens in the future depends on the accumulation of what has happened in the past – the history of the system matters.

Such feedback processes are an intrinsic component of self-organizing critical systems and are prevalent in contexts involving growth and evolution.

Whilst the study of such processes is still in its infancy, bringing these new tools to bear is dramatically extending our understanding of the Cosmos and is beginning to resolve deep mysteries relating to the Earth and its history. The insights they offer into the evolutionary and revolutionary aspects of collective influence and behaviour are also applicable to human interactions and social and economic systems.

Mem-branes

The same underlying holographic principles appear to operate throughout biological lifeforms, whether embodied by single-celled organisms or entire ecosystems. Modern biological research has emphasized the 'power' of genes and assumed that the more complex an organism, the greater the number of genes it would possess. However, the recent report of the Human Genome Project, which began in the late 1980s and sought to map the genetic sequence of human DNA, has astonished geneticists. For it has proven that not only do we have only about a quarter of the number of genes expected, but that there isn't much difference between that number and the gene count of much more primitive organisms. Clearly, genes are not the complete answer to the evolution of biological complexity!

A few pioneering biologists have, in contrast, focused on how an organism's relationship with its environment and, more specifically, its perception of its environment, directly control behaviour and gene activity, and thus ultimately evolution.

One of these scientists is cell biologist Bruce Lipton. Within a cell, the great majority of the genetic material is concentrated in the nucleus. Lipton has pointed out that if genes did represent the control centre or 'brain' of the cell, then taking out the nucleus would result in the cessation of all cell functions and ultimately the death of the cell. However, such enucleated cells are able to survive for several months, carrying on as normal by responding to environmental stimuli and continuing to sustain life. Lipton and others have concluded that it is instead the cell's membrane, its outer boundary and the only organ common to all living organisms, which represents its 'brain'.

As a semi-permeable barrier, the membrane enables the cell both to protect itself from the outer environment and to maintain control over its internal conditions. But it is not a passive boundary; it actively mediates information between its outer surroundings and the cell interior. It effectively controls adaptation by the recognition of environmental signals by 'receptor' proteins embedded within it. These perceive both physical signals, for example in the form of electrically charged chemical ions, and energetic signals such as those carried by electromagnetic vibrations.

It now appears that the maximum consciousness expressed throughout the physical universe may be proportional to the branes which are its holographic boundary. It also seems that the maximum perception able to be processed by a biological cell may be proportional to the surface area of its surrounding mem-brane.

The fractal evolution of multi-cellular organisms then enables increasing perception to be embodied. It thus optimizes the ability to adapt, survive and thrive and provides ever more abundant opportunities for conscious co-creation to unfold. All biological organisms, including humans, are thus essentially microcosmic holograms.

We all have causative templates for our physical forms, known as biofields. Research has also shown that the physical counterparts of these biofields are mediated by coherent electromagnetic fields, the *modus operandi* of the holographic principle.

In the same way that it is now being considered that fractal patterns may account for the evolution of life, systems theorists have discerned these patterns in the workings of human societies too. The rise and fall of economies, the incidence and scale of conflicts and the nature of the worldwide web all show that there is no fundamental difference between the 'natural' and 'man-made' world. They – and we – are all aspects of the cosmic hologram.

The Cosmic Hologram

We've now seen how science is being reconciled with spiritual tradition in the emerging perception of the holographic Cosmos.

Consciousness is progressively being viewed as an all-pervasive cosmic mind which is not only inherent at all scales of existence but *is* existence itself. The hologram of the physical world, expressing itself as energy that manifests as waves, is continually co-created from their interactions.

We now can appreciate that the universe is intrinsically interconnected and harmonic, and embodies underlying order and purpose. In so doing we can also begin to discern how we may align ourselves with our own higher purpose and the cosmic flow of life. We no longer need to struggle with the fragmented vision of the Cosmos that has come to dominate Western culture, for its view of the world is outdated and partial. We can now reclaim the deeper intuitive knowing that we are spiritual beings undergoing a physical experience and that at the most fundamental level we are all-one.

As we begin to acknowledge these deeper realities of space and time – and that our awareness can fly beyond their limitations – we are ready to begin our journey to re-member who we *really* are.

In the next chapter we'll explore the universal harmonics of light and sound that are intrinsic to the workings of the cosmic hologram. And we'll see their profound influence on our journeys as human beings.

CHAPTER 2

Harmonics of Creation

In the last chapter we explored how science is rediscovering what perennial wisdom has always maintained – that not only is the universe a holographic whole, but that it has creative purpose and meaning. In this chapter, we will focus on the harmonic attributes of light and sound. In their archetypal patterns we'll see how both wisdom teachings and science are revealing how consciousness expresses itself energetically throughout the resonant Cosmos.

Music

Fundamentally, as we've seen, it is the vibrating notes of minute strings from whose resonance all the energies of the universal hologram are believed to derive. The basic principles of creating music are the same principles by which consciousness co-creates the cosmic symphony of the universe. So the tenets of music and the numerical relationships from which its harmonies arise offer us the most appropriate language to describe how consciousness acts both within the physical world and on transcendental levels.

There are three elements of musical harmony that are crucial for our understanding of how consciousness co-creates the physical world.

Attunement

The first is that of attunement, which is the process of adjusting the frequency of something to harmonize with that of something else. This is revealed when we sound a tuning fork. When we do so, any stringed instrument nearby will automatically vibrate at the same note. Likewise, when we are 'in tune' with ourselves and with others, we are aligned with their frequency of vibration. Conversely, when we are 'out of tune' or dissonant, we are out of alignment. Our well-being, on mental, emotional and physical levels, actually depends on the extent to which we are energetically aligned and in harmony with all aspects of ourselves, each other and the wider world. The ancients understood that dis-ease arises from dis-harmony and were aware of the therapeutic benefits of light and sound.

Coherence

To understand the other two elements of harmony, we also need to appreciate that waveforms are not only described by their frequency but also their amplitude and phase.

As they travel, waveforms embody a three-in-one curve as each wave rises, peaks and falls away, every stage being a phase of the complete wave. Amplitude is the height of a wave from its midpoint – its intrinsic intensity or loudness.

With this understanding, we can now consider the second element of harmony, which is that of coherence. This describes a situation when not only the frequency but also the amplitude and phase of waveforms are aligned.

For example, the white light from a normal light bulb comprises many frequencies and amplitudes and is radiated in all directions, whereas the light of a laser has been attuned to a single frequency and direction and its waves aligned, peak to peak, in phase. The difference in focused power between the two is extraordinary. A light bulb can only be harnessed to illuminate a small space, whereas a laser is able to cut through metals. Indeed, a laser beam has been developed that is so powerful that it has recently been able to travel from Earth to intercept the *Messenger* satellite some 15 million miles away on its way to the planet Mercury.

Resonance

The third element of harmony is that of resonance, or sympathetic vibration. It occurs as a consequence of something being attuned to and thus coherent with something else and thereby the two combining their energies.

A well-known example of this was when the city of London celebrated the recent millennium by the opening of a new footbridge across the River Thames. As people began to walk across, it was discovered that the frequency of their footsteps was resonant with the bridge, causing it to sway dangerously. Only when its fundamental structure was altered and thus made dissonant from the walking frequency of its pedestrian users could it be used safely.

Resonance also occurs naturally when the frequencies that interact are octaves of each other. You may have noticed that when striking a note on a piano, the notes that are higher or lower octaves will also reverberate.

Our psyche may be likened to the octaves on a piano keyboard. When we undergo an experience, our perception of it resonates on the spiritual, mental, emotional and physical levels of our being. When our experiences are traumatic, if their energetic imprints are not resolved and released, they ultimately become chronic and may become embodied at cellular level as a physical dis-ease.

Co-creating Realities

These three primary elements of musical harmony –
attunement, coherence and resonance – also help us to
understand how we ultimately co-create our realities. For
when we intend to do something, we attune our attention to
it. Thus our awareness becomes coherent with our intention
and energetically resonant with that we intend. The greater
the intensity, or amplitude, of our intention and attention, the
more powerful the resonant energy and the manifestation of
our purpose.

The holographic nature of our consciousness is integral –
it is essentially different vibrations of a complete entity, our
soul. So, when we speak of intention and attention in this
way, it is important to understand that it may arise at any
level of our psyche, not only from the conscious awareness
of our ego-self but also from subconscious or transpersonal
levels of perception.

In the next chapter we'll discuss further how our beliefs and
perceptions shape our well-being and thus our lives. We shall
also continue to see how manifestation follows energy and how
energy expresses consciousness. This understanding is crucial
to our journey to embody the wholeness of who we really are.

Three-in-One

The holographic principle may be perceived as expressing
the One through the diversity of the many. All spiritual
teachings describe this sundering of unity consciousness into
universal polarities and depict it through various symbols.
It is, however, perhaps best known through the Taoist tradition
of yang and yin. Their ever-creative dance of active and
passive forces, light and shadow aspects, and male and female
attributes reverberates throughout all scales of existence.

But these active and passive forces can only create phenomena through the presence of a third principle, a neutral or creative force. Thus Taoist philosophy, in common with all perennial wisdom traditions, perceives that the innate nature of all manifestation is not two- but three-fold.

It is in the resolution of such three-in-one balance that the creativity of the One is explored. For example, night and day are balanced at dawn and dusk, and the sacred marriage of male and female principles is fertilized by the birth of a child.

Lama Kazi Dawa-Sandup describes how in Buddhist doctrine:

In the boundless panorama of the existing and visible universe, whatever shapes appear, whatever sounds vibrate, whatever radiances illuminate and whatever consciousness cognise, all are the play or manifestation of the Tri-kaya, the three-fold principle of the Cause of all causes, the primordial trinity.

Ultimately, on all symbolic, energetic and experiential levels, such three-in-oneness is fully expressed in the rising, peaking and falling away of waves. Whilst in their rising and falling the polarity expressions of yang and yin are overt, it is in the turning points when they peak and reform that the cycle is able to complete and move on, and it is through these turning points that all phenomena are co-created.

In the hologram, too, the unity of the initiating beam of light is split into two and it is only from the recombination of these two beams that the holographic image is born.

The Vedic tradition of ancient India also perceived the physical world, at its most profound level, as being continually created from the interplay of three fundamental principles of Nature, termed *gunas*. Translated as 'light', 'fire' (or 'creativity') and 'darkness', these three principles are all-pervasive, yet the ancient sages taught that light and darkness are unable to pair directly with each other. Creativity is needed to balance each with the other. Again, it is the third principle that is the moderator enabling resolution into wholeness.

In the writings of the Chinese *Tao Te Ching*, 'The Way of the Tao', or ultimate truth, the triadic nature of phenomena is symbolically described as:

The Tao begot One. One begat Two. Two begat Three.
And Three begat ten thousand things.
The ten thousand things carry yin and embrace yang.
They achieve harmony by combining these forces.

The Chinese recognized these cosmic combinations in archetypal tri-grams of yin and yang called *kua*. There are eight permutations of kua, from three yin to three yang and all variations in between.

The Chinese sage known as King Wen is credited with partnering two tri-grams to form a six-fold hexagram. His total of 64 possible combinations of these hexagrams comprise the divinatory tool of the *I Ching*, the 'Book of Changes'.

Millennia later, the mathematician Gottfried Leibniz saw in the *I Ching* the fundamental elements of the binary notation on which the language of computers is now based. And when the structure of DNA was discovered, it was found that the binary pairs of its genetic bases, or codons, were organized into the same matrix of 64 hexagrams as those of the *I Ching*.

Light

The three-in-one nature of phenomena is embodied in light itself. Visible light spans a single energetic octave within the electromagnetic spectrum. Over 70 octaves in its entirety, it ranges from high-frequency short-wavelength x-rays through microwaves to low-frequency long-wavelength radio waves and beyond. The intersection at 90 degrees of an electric and a magnetic field causes the waves of the electromagnetic spectrum to travel in a third, perpendicular direction. And at a fundamental level, as we discussed in the first chapter, light weaves together space and time itself.

The splitting of a beam of coherent light and its recombination is, as we've also seen, the basis of the hologram. But beams of coherent sound can also be created, split and recombined to form acoustic holograms. Indeed, dolphins create three-dimensional representations of their surroundings in this way.

The entire electromagnetic spectrum is intimately resonant with sound and the conversion between light and sound forms the basis of our global technologies. For example, when I pick up a telephone to make a call, the sound of my voice is converted to a digital signal which is then transmitted as electromagnetic energy down the phone line or beamed via a satellite to the telephone of the person I'm calling. When they pick up their phone, my voice is then reconverted to sound in their receiver. And when they speak, their voice reaches me through the same alchemical process.

Biofields

The ancients perceived the interplay of cosmic light and sound as forming the supra-physical templates of manifest forms. Research is now revealing that coherent electromagnetic fields are the ordering principle for our physical body. The energetic template for the physical structure of an organism is generally known as its 'biofield', although biologist Rupert Sheldrake has also coined the term 'morphic field'.

Research is indicating that there may be higher-dimensional attributes of electromagnetic fields and these may form the basis of such biofields. They may be mediated into material form by the physical components of such coherent fields.

Pioneering research into the low-energy fields of the body support this idea. The molecular structure both within and between the cells of our body is sufficiently ordered to support the semi-conduction of electricity. The uniform polarity of our nerves acts as one-way wave-guides for electromagnetic pulses, giving energetic coherence to our nervous system.

Electrical fields in the outer layer of the membrane of our skin also appear to initiate regrowth by stimulating cell differentiation and thus healing. Electrical fields are intrinsically involved too in the process by which cells change to and from being functionally specialized and thus in how the diversity of physical form is realized.

Sound

As the harmonics of coherent light form the holographic template for our physical form, we shouldn't be surprised that the harmonies of sound are also essential to our mental, emotional and physical well-being.

By the age of 24 weeks, the ears of a human foetus are fully formed and its responsiveness to sound amply proven.

It is now becoming commonplace for expectant mothers to play music to babies in the womb. The sound of normal heartbeats also soothes newborns to sleep, whereas an accelerated heartbeat or dissonant sound will upset them.

Experiments with plants have also shown that playing music to them will accelerate or inhibit normal growth, depending on the type of music chosen. Classical or devotional music has been proven to have beneficial effects, while rock music has been shown to have the opposite impact.

Such experiments with plants demonstrate that regardless of our own personal musical likes and dislikes, on an objective level, different tonalities of music have different effects on biological well-being.

One of the most significant findings of botanist Dr T. C. Singh has been that later generations of the seeds of plants musically stimulated by beneficial music continue to display the improved traits. While there has been no such verified experimentation with plants exposed to disruptive music, it would be logical that negative traits would also be transferred on a generational basis.

Indeed, biologists are beginning to recognize that such so-called 'epigenetic traits', which are also a consequence of lifestyle and environment, are a significant factor in our own genetic inheritance too.

Hear and Listen

Hearing is the first sense to develop *in utero* and appears to be the last to fade as we approach the demise of our physical body. How we hear has a profound effect on how we learn and how we interact with the outside world.

Medical doctor Alfred Tomatis, who has made a lifetime

study of hearing, makes a clear distinction between hearing and listening. He defines hearing as a passive process where we merely detect the sounds around us. Listening, on the other hand, is an active process requiring the conscious intention to understand the meaning of what we are hearing. As a consequence, we may enjoy excellent hearing but be poor listeners.

The study of sensory integration pioneered by Jean Ayres has also shown that when the vestibule of the inner ear is under-stimulated, children can become hyperactive as they attempt to compensate for their lack of auditory stimulation.

To become good listeners we not only need to be able to hear the sound and focus on the information embedded in it but also to be able to filter out unnecessary background noise. Whilst good listeners can tune in and out of sonic awareness, poor listeners don't have the ability to selectively tune out. In extremis, their only defence mechanism against continuous bombardment is to tune out all sound. That is what ADD (Attention Deficit Disorder) individuals do.

But we hear not only through our ears, for sound is also conducted through the bones of our body. If, for whatever reason, this inner sound is tuned out, we also find learning difficult.

Tomatis and other researchers have discovered that people with ADHD (Attention Deficit Hyperactive Disorder) or ADD, especially children, listen too much with their bodies and don't have a way to selectively filter such sensory information – they either pay attention to all input or screen everything out. If they pay attention to everything, they are unable to focus on any given topic and thus appear to have a deficit of attention. They also feel overwhelmed and become frustrated, angry or anxious. Conversely, screening everything out results in lethargy and withdrawal.

Over many years Tomatis and his colleagues have developed powerful techniques that retrain the ears to become the primary gatekeepers of sound for the body. By desensitizing bone conduction stress is reduced and listening and learning are supported.

Tomatis has also discovered that we hear differently through each ear and that everyone is either right-ear or left-ear dominant. Those of us who are right-ear dominant are generally able to learn more easily than those whose dominant ear is their left. This is logical, given that our right ear connects directly with the left hemisphere of our brain, which is primarily responsible for the development and processing of language. With left-ear dominance, the signals connect directly with the right brain but must then be relayed to the left brain for language processing. Not only does this slow down information processing, but certain higher frequencies of sound are lost in the transfer. Such ear dominance thus not only influences our ability to learn language-based skills but also affects our ability to communicate and thus our emotional well-being.

Again, Tomatis has developed ways of alleviating extremes of such imbalance. However, music is associated with the right hemisphere of the brain and thus the left ear. Whilst I'm not aware that any research has yet been undertaken, I feel it would be useful to test whether left-ear dominance can be correlated with musical ability.

Our ears also amazingly act as a relay station for *all* sensory information between the nervous system and the brain. As such, not only our hearing but also our vision and sense of touch are mediated through the mechanism of the ear. So learning and other behavioural difficulties may be far more due to listening difficulties than is commonly recognized. However, as Tomatis's techniques have shown, in very many cases they may be alleviated.

Entrainment

As musicologist David Tame has noted, it is likely that music, like language, gives us a framework of mental concepts and emotional experiences with which to mould our view of the world.

Indeed, language profoundly affects the way we perceive the world around us. Tame has pointed out that when a society has no word for a particular concept, it is often unable to identify its reality. He reports the inability of some African tribes to distinguish colours for which they have no name, even though their eyesight is perfectly normal.

The words of a language encode concepts and phenomena that are culturally perceived and experienced. In childhood the adoption of our native language effectively entrains our thoughts.

But music not only entrains our thoughts, but also our emotions and bodies on conscious and subconscious levels. As musicologist Julius Portnoy discovered, by affecting our mental and emotional states it is also able to change our metabolism, raise or lower our blood pressure and influence our digestion.

What Portnoy found was that music whose rhythm is about the same rate as our normal heartbeat will soothe us. When it is slower, we will feel suspense, and when it is faster, we feel excited.

There are now hundreds of studies on the effects of music, especially when allied to powerful visual imagery, and all show a link between media violence and anti-social behaviour. Whilst language correlates with our left brain of mental conceptualization, music does so with the right brain of emotional perception. It effectively transcends spoken language and resonates directly with our emotions. As such its power – for good or ill – is enormous.

Music Therapy

Ancient healing techniques relied substantially on the therapeutic value of music to soothe. Much of the inspirational influence of the Vedic and Greek sagas derived from their being sung rather than spoken. In recent years, there has been a resurgence in sound therapy, led by practitioners such as Don Campbell, Jonathan Goldman and James D'Angelo.

All such therapies extol the value of waves of sound interwoven with waves of silence. In the Vedic tradition of ancient India, whose Sanskrit texts are probably the earliest written source of ancient wisdom, audible sound is either *ahata*, the physical expression of cosmic sound, or *anahata*. Whilst the former is heard by the ears, the latter can only be 'heard' in communion with transcendental realities.

Anahata is also the name given by the same tradition to the heart chakra – recognizing that it is the heart that hears the archetypal Word of God.

The ancient Egyptian name for the imminent creator was Amn, from which the 'amen' of Christian prayers derives. Amn is also associated with the cosmic sound or Word of the Vedic sages, the *Aum* or *Om*. Not only does the *A-u-m* thus represent the primal sound of the Cosmos, but also by uttering it, especially as an integral part of a spiritual practice such as yoga, one is deemed to be in alignment and harmony with the cosmic flow.

Binaural Beats

When we hear sounds of nearly the same frequency as each other in stereo – with different signals reaching each ear – our brain integrates the two and produces the sensation of a third sound called a 'binaural beat'.

The signals may be chosen so that the frequency of the binaural beat is low and within the range of brainwave frequencies. The Monroe Institute in Virginia, founded by Robert Monroe and now led by his daughter Laurie, has developed powerful techniques of mixing filtered white noise (known as 'pink noise') with binaural beats of specific frequencies to facilitate states of focused consciousness. The Institute has recorded CDs of so-called 'metamusic' that combines musical compositions with underlying binaural beats. These variously promote states of relaxation and meditation conducive to healing, peak states which aid learning and creativity, and mystical states which access our higher awareness.

The Power of Music

That the ancients appreciated the power of music and its ability to engender altered states of consciousness is also clear from the multitude of sacred monuments around the world whose structures and geometries are acoustically resonant. From the sonic niches at the temple of Ollantaytambo, Peru, to the pyramids of Egypt, the Treasury of Atreus in Greece and the Neolithic chambered monuments of Britain, the ancient world was replete with sanctuaries of sound. The soaring architecture of the Gothic cathedrals of mediaeval Europe, too, is essentially music frozen in stone.

The primacy of cosmic sound was of major cosmological

significance to the dynasties of ancient China. The foundation tone for their imperial music, the *huang chung*, or 'yellow bell', was reset by each incoming emperor to ensure alignment between Heaven and Earth. This purest manifestation of the creative impulse of the Cosmos was used to ensure that all Chinese music fulfilled its sole purpose: to purify both performers and listeners and align them with divine will.

Such a consciously creative role for music, for good or ill, has also been utilized in both free and totalitarian societies. For example, as David Tame relates, when Stalin came to power in the USSR, he immediately understood that the hitherto liberal approach to music posed a significant threat to communist rule, for the musical forms that had developed had increasingly encouraged individual expression. Accordingly, he strengthened the authority of the conservative Russian Association of Proletarian Musicians, which derided any music remotely progressive and thereby ensured that music adhered to the political will of the state.

The Chromatic Scale

The vast compendium of musical expression across all cultures and throughout history is in its entirety made up of only 13 notes. All music, from Vedic mantras to Mozart sonatas to Beatles ballads, is composed of the 12 notes of the chromatic musical scale, the 13th of which both completes one octave and begins the next.

Within the completeness of the chromatic scale, the ancients identified two sub-scales, which form the basis for the prevailing Western and Eastern musical traditions. The diatonic scale, which completes the octave on the eighth note, is familiar to us as the white notes on a piano. And throughout Asia, the pentatonic scale is made up of five notes that also span an octave.

The Greek philosopher Pythagoras was the first to teach the principles of the chromatic scale outside the temples of ancient Egypt, Chaldea and India. The notes of the scale are based on fundamental ratios of simple whole numbers and the creation of the complete scale begins with a string, or wire, of any length fixed at both ends to a stable base and pulled taut, as in a guitar or violin. When the string is stroked, it will vibrate at its fundamental note, which is dependent on its length. Placing a finger or bridge at the halfway point of the string will produce a note which, when either half-length is stroked, is twice the frequency of the fundamental note – the interval known as the octave. Dividing the string at two-thirds of its length thus creates two notes an octave apart. By then continuing to divide each two-thirds section into an ever-smaller sequence of two-thirds ratios, a range of higher notes is produced, each in a harmonious relationship with the ones before and after. On the 13th step, the cycle is completed when the original note is sounded once more, although slightly flat.

This chromatic scale of the ancients is harmonically resonant with the physiology of the spiral of our inner ear and also with our body as a whole. The white and black notes of the modern piano represent it, but with one crucial difference. For between the actual 13th note and the ideal doubling there is a small difference in frequency – 1.34 per cent – which was known to the ancients and is termed the 'comma of Pythagoras'. The initiates of this Greek master recognized that the open spiralling to ever-higher frequencies enabled by the comma embodied the evolution innate to the physical world. They may also have understood that the harmonic of 12 into 13 is the fundamental means by which unity consciousness is embodied in physical form.

With the introductions of orchestras in the 17th century, however, the difficulty of tuning between different instruments resulted in the introduction of the even-tempered scale used today. Now the difference represented by the comma of Pythagoras is evenly distributed across the 12 notes of the scale, ensuring that the 13th is an exact octave – or doubling – above the first.

Whilst pragmatic, this modern adjustment has moved away from the musical harmony with which our bodies are naturally resonant. But these ancient rhythms and the therapeutic nature of music are now returning to our consciousness as we seek the re-establishment of well-being, harmony and wholeness.

Cymatics

The innate musicality and harmony of Nature was also revealed to the German physicist Ernst Chladni 200 years ago. Chladni discovered that when he covered a flat metal plate with a thin layer of sand and stroked the plate with a bow, rather like playing a violin, visible patterns appeared in the sand.

More recently, Swiss doctor Hans Jenny expanded on Chladni's ideas by using a variety of media to demonstrate the primacy of vibration to all physical forms. He called this process 'cymatics', from the Greek word for 'wave', *kyma*.

In the ancient science of sacred architecture, the most fundamental geometric harmonics revealed through cymatics were incorporated into the dimensions and shapes of buildings which were created as microcosms of the cosmic symphony, to ease and heal the body and free the spirit.

Harmonics of Creation

In our exploration of cosmic light and sound, we have discovered that consciousness co-creates the cosmic symphony of the universe using the same harmonic principles that are innate to musical expression. These fundamental harmonics of creation continually sound throughout the Cosmos. Intention and awareness then manifest our realities through the harmonic principles of attunement, coherence and resonance.

In future chapters we'll see how the 13 notes of the musical scale are intrinsic to understanding the wholeness of our soul. And as we expand our awareness, we shall raise the vibrations of our consciousness to ever-greater flights of Spirit.

In the next chapter we shall indeed fly beyond the confines of space and time.

CHAPTER 3

Believing Is Seeing

The emerging awareness of the holographic Cosmos is poised to eliminate the apparent separation of matter and mind that has been the basis of the schism between science and Spirit for so long. For the consciousness of the cosmic mind is primary to its universal expression as energy, and all matter – including our physical body – is formed by the standing waves of coherent energies.

Intelligence thus pervades our entire physical body. Whilst specific organs, such as the brain, have their individual functional purposes and specialities, the body as a whole is a microcosmic hologram that processes and memorizes the experiences of our human personality.

Memory, emotions and perception are thus embodied at cellular levels. And whilst the brain is the primary processor of our ego consciousness, other levels of awareness, including the responses and habitual patterns of our subconscious, are distributed throughout the entirety of our body.

The Holographic Body

It now seems evident that our higher energetic template, our biofield, is mediated into physical form by coherent electromagnetic fields.

In the earliest stages of a human embryo, as indeed for all biological organisms, every gene of our DNA is fully active and every cell is like every other. These primary, or stem, cells then begin to form three rudimentary tissue layers, or membranes – the projection screens of our holographic consciousness.

As the organism develops further, some of the available genes start to deactivate and new cells become specialized. The inner membrane, or endoderm, grows into the glands and viscera of our body. The middle, or mesoderm, becomes our bones, muscles and circulatory system. And the outer, ectoderm, develops into our skin, sense organs and nervous system.

And after nine months, the microcosmic hologram that is the vessel for our soul's journey in its current life is born.

Integral Mind

To describe consciousness and matter as separate is as nonsensical as talking of the waves of the ocean as being separate from the ocean itself. Mind is integral, with different levels of awareness that may be likened to the frequencies of electromagnetic energies. For example, whilst radio waves vibrate at lower frequencies than visible light, which in turn vibrate at lower frequencies than x-rays, all form part of a continuing spectrum.

But just as with the electromagnetic spectrum, where different frequencies have different attributes, so it is with our integrated mind. Essentially our subconscious awareness vibrates at different frequencies from our waking consciousness – our ego-mind. And we are also innately connected with many other levels of consciousness above that which we delineate as our personality.

However, the purpose of our ego-self is to embody a personality and experience the creativity of our human journey. So, rather like a method actor in a play, the role of our ego-mind is to fully immerse us in the reality of our physical life. To do so, it perceives its individual self to be separate from the wider world.

Our heart knows better. Whereas the role of our ego-mind is to separate, the role of our heart – our feelings – is to unite.

And ultimately, the role of our will is to reconcile these two parental influences and to meld them into the creativity and learning that are our human experience.

The Stage of Life

The physical realm has long been considered by metaphysicians to offer us the most profound and challenging opportunities to explore the cosmic polarities of light and shadow, male and female, love and fear, and ultimately to embrace their resolution.

It has also been described as a stage. As Shakespeare claimed in *As You Like It*, 'All the world's a stage and all the men and women merely players…'

We may indeed perceive that ultimately we are actors on the stage of life. And just as actors take off their costume and go home at the end of their performance, so do we. For the great majority of us, the method acting of our ego-self means that we do this only at the end of our lives – or indeed afterwards. But during our life, we can choose to see beyond the physical stage and comprehend who we *really* are. And as we do so we come to understand that in the play of our life, we are the ultimate co-author.

Whilst this has been the quest of spiritual seekers from time immemorial, individually and collectively we are now living in momentous times when such awareness is available to all of us. We are living in a time when we are able to expand our consciousness beyond the limitations of our ego-self and offer ourselves the opportunity to embody our highest purpose.

Believing Is Seeing

Generally, the ego-self is culturally conditioned. Therefore it not only acts in accordance with the prevailing world-view and beliefs, but it is literally unable to see what it cannot imagine. In essence, there is no resonance on that basis and so the ego-self has no way of attuning itself to new and effectively unimaginable phenomena.

A few years ago, an experiment in perception at the University of Illinois demonstrated this. Volunteers were shown the video of a basketball game during which a woman in a gorilla suit walked across the court. When the volunteers were asked afterwards if they had noticed anything unusual, most of them had completely missed the unscheduled appearance of the gorilla.

However, where our ego-self can imagine a phenomenon and believes in or is at least open to its reality, we are able to directly experience and essentially co-create that reality.

The old adage of 'seeing is believing' is now being shown to be back to front, for it is rather the case that 'believing is seeing'.

In Chapter 1, we saw how research into what is being called the 'New Biology' is determining how our perceptions directly affect our biology both on conscious and subconscious levels. There we discussed the emerging model of the cell membrane as an organic information processor which is dynamically interlinked with the environment. And we discussed how the behaviour and internal conditions of the cell reflect the recognition of perceived environmental stimuli – both physical *and* energetic.

But such awareness may be distorted, only partially understood or even completely incorrect. It represents our beliefs about reality, rather than its actuality. So, thought processes and emotions, whether 'true' or otherwise, influence the behaviour of our cells. Accordingly, our mental and emotional convictions – on both conscious and subliminal levels – are able to influence our physical body, guiding it to health or dis-ease.

The beliefs about ourselves which we develop during our formative years are especially powerful in the imprinting of subconscious and habitual patterns of behaviour. Such patterns may limit and blight our entire lives unless we seek to understand and heal them.

Love, Joy and Gratitude

It's not only the way we think and act but also the way that we feel that makes us who we are. Our ego-mind persuades us of our individuality, but our heart re-members that we are ultimately all-one. If we allow it, our heart unites us.

It can only do so, however, if it is open. For many of us, including myself for much of my earlier life, our mind convinces us that the pain of emotional trauma will cease only if we stop feeling. At the age of 20, I shut down my heart. I thought this was my refuge, but it was actually a prison of my own making. And it took me a further 25 years to break down the prison walls I had erected.

In later chapters we'll explore not only the reasons why we harm ourselves in such ways, but also how to understand and release such traumatic imprints.

Biologists have also now recognized that the heart has its own nervous system and that a two-way bio-communication system operates between the heart and the brain.

Indeed, as we develop in our mother's womb, our heart begins to beat before our brain starts to form. Even then, it is the part of the brain that relates to emotions that grows first and only afterwards that the 'thinking' part develops.

The primary role of our heart significantly affects how we interact with the world. Research has shown that success in life, as measured using both material criteria and the quality of our experience, appears to depend far more on our ability to develop our emotional intelligence than on our intellectual prowess.

Other studies have demonstrated that regardless of educational opportunities, our intellect is relatively fixed from childhood. Our emotional intelligence, however, can develop throughout our entire life, provided we are prepared to 'live and learn'.

Our emotional well-being has significant influence too on both our physical health and indeed longevity. For over 15 years, stress researchers at the HeartMath Institute in California have amassed experimental findings that conclusively demonstrate that negative emotions such as insecurity, anger and fear throw our nervous system out of balance and cause heart rhythms that are jagged and disordered. The positive emotions of love, joy and gratitude, however, create coherent energy signals that increase order, reduce stress, bring balance throughout our nervous system and are reflected in harmonious rhythms of our hearts.

Sensitives, mediums and dowsers also have a wealth of anecdotes and case studies testifying to the same findings. And there is now substantial scientific evidence that shows that when we enhance our emotional intelligence and invoke the intuitive wisdom of our heart, we send energetic signals to every cell of our body, restoring balance and well-being.

Sixth and Seventh Senses

Our mind, emotions and physical body essentially 'see' what we believe about the world around us and ourselves. But research into consciousness is also proving that we have additional ways of 'seeing' that our ego-mind often chooses to ignore.

In Chapter 1, we introduced the phenomenon of nonlocality, spontaneous communication that transcends spacetime. Not only have physicists proven its reality at quantum levels but researchers investigating human consciousness have also revealed that we have the innate ability to perceive and influence events nonlocally, or 'at a distance'.

Experiments have shown that both humans and animals are able to detect much more subtle environmental signals and electromagnetic influences that had hitherto been undetected. Often these affect us at subliminal levels and are now being recognized as contributing to what has been known as our 'sixth' sense.

However, we need to differentiate this sensitivity to influences that we are still able to pick up at a sensory level from the true nonlocal awareness of our 'seventh sense'. And whilst traditional evolutionary theory has been able to suggest survival benefits and thus reasons for the evolution of our sixth sense, there is no such explanation, other than the primacy of consciousness, for our seventh.

Influence 'at a Distance'

The investigation of nonlocal perception, such as telepathy, across both space and time has been at the cutting edge of consciousness research for the last three decades. By 1995 sufficient evidence had been amassed for the U.S. Congress to request the American Institutes for Research (AIR) to review government-sponsored studies of such psi phenomena as remote viewing, commissioned by the CIA.

The report of the AIR clearly stated that the statistical results obtained by the experiments were far beyond those expected by chance. Having reviewed the integrity of the experimental protocols, they refuted any possibility that the results could be due to any flaws in the methods used and also confirmed that the results had been replicated at a number of laboratories around the world. They concluded that the reality of the phenomena was proven. Their recommendation was that rather than continuing to experiment merely to offer further proof of the existence of psi, future research should focus on understanding how the phenomena work and developing practical applications.

Whilst in the West psi research has been significantly held back by the closed attitudes of most institutions and scientists, such limitations have not been imposed elsewhere. In Russia, for example, the State Universities of Moscow and St Petersburg and the Russian and Ukraine Academies of Sciences have long supported such enquiries.

In recent years, however, a growing number of Western universities and institutions have been supporting psi research and there are now well-established parapsychology departments in the UK, including the Koestler Parapsychology Unit (KPU) at the University of Edinburgh, the Centre for the Study of Anomalous Psychological Processes (CSAPP) at University College, Northampton, and the Mind-Matter Unification Project led by Nobel Laureate Brian Josephson at the Cavendish Laboratory of Cambridge University.

In the U.S., too, the Consciousness Research Laboratory (CRL) at the University of Nevada, the PEAR Laboratory at Princeton University and the Department of Psychology of the University of Arizona are pioneers of such studies. A number of other organizations, including the Institute of Noetic Sciences in San Francisco founded by former astronaut Edgar Mitchell, the Rhine Research Center in North Carolina and the Boundary Institute in California, also continue to undertake such leading-edge research.

Awareness and Influence

Psi phenomena are generally classified into those phenomena involving passive awareness and those incorporating active influence.

Passive nonlocal perception includes the remote viewing of distant locations, where a person can attune to circumstances or events occurring in another place or even another time. Conversely, active influence 'at a distance' is encountered in such phenomena as telepathy, where one person can mentally communicate with another, and in the ability to affect the outcome of ostensibly random events.

In my book *The Wave,* I detail the sorts of experiments that are convincing ever more people that psi phenomena are both real and an innate aspect of our nature. Here we'll focus on a number of findings that have important implications for the ways in which we co-create our realities.

Our normal waking perception is generally occupied with processing the awareness of the outer world that we receive through our five physical senses, especially our eyes and ears. The quieter messages of our sixth sense and the nonlocal awareness of our seventh are thus usually drowned out by the sensory noise around us.

To reduce such 'noise' and thus enhance our psychic sensitivity, spiritual traditions have for millennia sought outer peace and quiet combined with altered states of consciousness involving an alert and receptive mind. To investigate psi effects, researchers have developed similar techniques of sensory deprivation, termed the *Ganzfeld*, a German word meaning 'whole field', to induce such states. These experiments have confirmed the benefit of such conditions in enhancing psi receptivity.

Investigations into passive perception in the 1970s and 1980s showed them that only a small percentage of tested volunteers displayed consistent aptitude and apparently that neither training nor practice significantly improved the performance of the others. Conversely, experiments into active psi phenomena, such as telepathy, have shown that both practice and feedback improve a person's future performance.

So whilst it seems from the vast array of experiments that our ability to both transmit and receive nonlocal information is innate, the occurrence of ultra-sensitive psi perception, at least currently, is relatively rare.

But, as telepathic experiments have confirmed, feedback that encourages our ego-mind to relax and accept the validity of such perception enables us to improve our conscious ability to do so. And ongoing research is updating and improving the means by which such psi abilities can be nurtured and expanded. For in addition to the many organizations already mentioned, a growing number of institutions, such as the College of Psychic Studies in London, offer ongoing training in developing such psychic and intuitive awareness.

The experiments we have reviewed to date have considered both 'at a distance' passive perception and active influence between individuals. But, as we have seen, the holographic principle describes a Cosmos that is wholly interconnected at all scales of existence. So, what is the evidence for our collective influence?

Collective Responses

Over the last 15 years, experiments have conclusively proven that at peak moments of group attention, both at conscious and unconscious levels, we are able to change the random outcome of events.

The ongoing Global Consciousness Project, comprising over 70 researchers around the world, was set up in 1998. It seeks to study the influence of collective human consciousness through the large-scale sharing of reactions to major news events. For those events that invoke a shared coherent and intense response at a specific time or over a relatively short period, the influence has been seen to be significant, as was the case both with the events of 11 September 2001 in New York and Washington and the funeral of Pope John Paul II on 8 April 2005.

Given that the level of influence appears to increase with coherent intensity, such as an outpouring of compassion at a specific event or moment in time, then an event that elicited varied or variable reactions or which occurred over an extended period of time would be likely to reduce the level of coherence and thus the corresponding level of influence. This was seen by the Project's measurement of the global response to the tsunami of 26 December 2004. The nonlocal influence here was muted, but the fact that the appalling extent of the disaster only became apparent over the course of a number of days may be the cause of its reduced nonlocal impact.

Nonlocal Healing

Another series of studies has sought to investigate the phenomenon of distant healing, which has been linked with the spontaneous remission of illnesses, the alleviation of pain and the accelerated recovery of many patients around the world.

From a scientific perspective, such studies are extremely difficult to evaluate, due to the great number of associated variables. However, the evidence accumulated over many years by researchers such as psychologist William Braud and anthropologist Marilyn Schlitz has conclusively determined that people are able to consciously influence the nervous system of remote participants and affect their blood pressure, muscle response and skin conductivity.

What is consistently reported in such studies is that the efficacy of the healing depends on the healers being at least open to a higher power working through them, although the specific beliefs and spiritual traditions of the individual healers appear to be irrelevant. A key requirement is that the healers are not personally attached to the outcome of the healing influence. Perhaps the message to all healers should be 'Let e-go and let God.'

Co-creation

All these experiments demonstrate our ability not only to perceive on nonlocal spatial and temporal levels but also to influence apparently random events. Their cumulative results are undeniably far beyond chance and demonstrate what metaphysical traditions have always maintained – that we individually and collectively co-create our realities.

In scientific terms, the resonance of our attention and intention – and also that of our subconscious patterning – causes the quantum field of free-wave possibilities to harmonize into the coherent standing waves of real-ized materiality.

And, as we shall see, the higher our vibrational awareness, the more focused our attention and the more coherent our intention, the greater our empowerment to consciously co-create sustained health and well-being.

Ego

During our waking hours, we are generally aware of the self-consciousness we call the ego. It is this self which seems separate from others – it has a defined personality, a human history and a cultural heritage and affiliation.

Both on conscious and subconscious levels, we are continually interpreting our body's sensory communication and interaction with our external environment. It is primarily by such perception that our psyche derives its sense of material individuality and ongoing sense of ego-self. However, all such sensory information is filtered through the lens of cultural conditioning and defined by the individual personality. So it is the combination of our conscious mind and our habitual subconscious patterns which prejudges the possibility of nonlocal consciousness and psi effects and thus delineates what we consider to be 'real'. In altered states of consciousness, where the sensory distractions and boundaries of our conscious perception are relaxed, the mind is enabled to expand and explore such nonlocal and other levels of awareness and to let go of its attachment to the narrow confines of the ego.

Coherence

Coherence is integral to the phenomenon of nonlocality. On a quantum level, nonlocal connections between 'twin', or entangled, particles, which behave as a single entity throughout both space *and* time, are generated in a number of ways. But each technique crucially requires the coherence of the originating energy patterns.

One method raises a group of atoms to exactly the same level of energetic excitement. On returning to their naturally stable state, they release coherent energy in the form of twin particles. Another technique involves the use of lasers to create such entangled pairs.

Similarly, when at some level of awareness our psyche is coherently attuned, we too can both perceive and exert influence on such levels that transcend space and time. For most people the filter of the ego-mind tends to shut out the possibility of such phenomena. However, as we become open to the possibility of such awareness, the tight grip of our ego-mind loosens and we can access such comprehension on the level of full waking consciousness or in the alert state of light trance. Whilst some people are naturally gifted in this way, we all have the ability to perceive nonlocally.

How could it be otherwise, for this is our true nature!

Attunement

Unsurprisingly, given the underlying resonance throughout the holographic Cosmos, psi experiments have shown that when we are coherent – when we are attuned to or on the same energetic wavelength as something or someone else – our ability to perceive and communicate 'at a distance' is significantly enhanced.

This is like the difference between switching on an untuned radio and hearing just 'noise' – which is actually the background sound of deep space – and actively tuning in to a particular radio station and being able to hear the programme it is transmitting.

We ourselves are continually both transmitting and receiving – it's just that most of us aren't aware of it. Our abilities to attune to the Cosmos, whether to our own highest awareness, to empathize with others, to find lost keys or to discover underground water, are all aspects of our inherent nature. And the more we practise attunement, the greater our ability to do so.

Assuming that someone is open to the possibility of consciously accessing their nonlocal awareness, there are three crucial requirements which enable most people to do so. These are a relaxed body, an open mind and a peaceful heart.

As the *Ganzfeld* method has demonstrated, our psi abilities are enhanced when we are inwardly and outwardly quiet and our awareness is not bombarded by the myriad sensations and environmental signals we encounter on an everyday basis.

Not all of us have access to the stringent laboratory conditions of such quietude, but the aim is to be relaxed yet open and alert and in a light meditative state, so a quiet room, a comfortable chair and low lighting are helpful for most people. Too comfortable a chair is liable to send us to sleep, however! A dining-room chair or similar is usually best, as it supports a sitting position with our head, neck and back straight, our hands resting lightly on our legs above the knee and both feet flat and balanced on the floor.

Trying to attune when we are emotionally disturbed can be very difficult. So before beginning a session, aim to be calm. If you are feeling upset, there is a breath exercise on page 243 which you may find helpful.

For most of us, the most difficult thing to quieten is what the yogic initiates of ancient India called our 'monkey-mind'. This is the insistent way in which our waking egoic consciousness darts here and there in a continual inner dialogue, fomenting ideas, passing judgements and processing the experiences of our everyday life. Here, too, most spiritual traditions emphasize breathing techniques like the one offered in this book. What I have personally found most helpful is not to try to deny the monkey-mind thoughts as they arise, nor to judge them or force them away, but to allow them to flow away effortlessly by focusing on the in- and out-breath.

Like all practices, the more you do it, the easier it gets. But I don't know anyone, however long they have undertaken such practice, who doesn't experience the ongoing mischief of the monkey-mind, so don't allow yourself to be too troubled by it.

Modes of Perception

Awareness at a distance, as we have seen, is both passive and active. We can attune to such perception with the aim of receiving information, as is the case in remote viewing, or we can actively seek to influence on such levels, for instance to communicate telepathically or to offer others healing or the support of our prayers.

In both passive and active modes of awareness, we each have different and preferred means of perception. Some of us visualize on an inner level. Others feel or sense something. Yet others may hear sounds or smell fragrances. A few busy people are able to multi-task and psychically pick up on all these levels. And sometimes we just know! None of these ways is better than any of the others – they are all just more or less effective for us.

Sometimes, as we become more practised, not only is our initial mode of awareness enhanced but we also begin to perceive in other ways too. For example, if our primary mode of nonlocal awareness is to feel impressions, we may find ourselves beginning to visualize too, and vice versa.

Such higher attunement takes time and effort and, as with so many things, greater commitment to practice will almost inevitably result in faster progress. The progress of our spiritual alignment also walks hand in hand with our commitment to an inner journey of insight, healing and growth.

Believing Is Seeing

As we've seen, our bodies are microcosmic holograms, the vessels for our integral consciousness to explore what it means to be human. Our ego-mind, emotions and body thus 'see' what we believe about ourselves and the wider world. But even if our cultural conditioning is such that our ego-mind has a purely materialistic world-view, our heart and our body know better.

We've seen how our awareness is intrinsically nonlocal and that at last science too is recognizing the realities of such psi phenomena as telepathy and distant healing. As our awareness expands, individually and collectively we are beginning to see the Cosmos more clearly and access our 8th and higher chakras. We have already begun the journey to wholeness.

In the next chapter we'll see how an octave of eight cosmic principles enables consciousness to explore its ever-creative expression and we'll delve more deeply into the nature of time and explore what we mean by free will and destiny.

CHAPTER 4

Cosmic Principles

The holographic universe is exquisitely set up to enable consciousness to express itself through polarity-based awareness and ultimately to bring it to resolution. And as everything within the universe is related to everything else, all that we experience within the physical world is based on such real-ativity.

The personality of our ego-self is also continually exploring the relationships between our thoughts, feelings and senses. Their ever-changing dynamic forms the creative dance of our inner experiences. And in our outer relationships with others and the wider world, the microcosm of our inner self resonates holographically on ever-larger scales of our collective co-creation.

Space and Time

The fundamental nature of spacetime is, as we have seen, understood by science to be essentially a universal DVD. Every point of spacetime is considered to co-exist all at once, and it is only our mind that creates the perception of the flow of time and the unfolding of events.

We may then liken our consciousness to a cosmic DVD player which, through our coherent attention and intention, is able to express and store the diversity of our individual and collective experiences of what we term the 'physical world'.

Sensing the flow of time and the universal arrow of its direction is essential for our experiences of the physical world – for choices to be made and their implications to unfold. Our nonlocal awareness, however, transcends the limitations of spacetime, though it seems to do so with certain limitations. These may hold the key to a deeper understanding of time and its purpose.

Creation in the Now

To begin to understand the holographic universe, we need to perceive the metaphysical intention behind its creation. In a hologram, a coherent beam of light is split into two and recombined to form a holographic image. With the universe, it appears that it is a beam of coherent intention of consciousness that is split into two. One beam embodies the totality of what we call the past and the other beam the ongoing intention of consciousness that forms the future. They meet in the present moment that we call the Now. And thus it is only in the Now that the holographic universe is actually created.

The fundamental fabric of spacetime – past, present and future – exists in its entirety, as maintained by physicists. But information relating to the accumulation of all the events we call the 'past' appears to be imprinted on what the ancient sages called the 'Akashic Record' and what cosmologists now refer to as the 'zero-point field'. In this model, future events flow towards us from the higher intention of consciousness mediated by the second holographic beam. Essentially the future is not yet fully formed, but continues to be co-created in every moment.

Nonlocal awareness seems to support this emerging view of the physical world. And, as discussed in *The Wave*, experiments have shown that we are indeed able to have precognition of the future. The experience of such awareness suggests too that the future continues to crystallize until it becomes the co-created Now. We are thus able to have more complete nonlocal perception of the past, by accessing the Akashic Record, than we are to perceive a still-forming 'future'.

The focus, or coherence, of conscious intention is the means by which the waves of probability of the quantum field are manifested and actualized in the standing waves of specific outcomes – the energies/matter we call physical reality. So when we perceive the 'future' during precognition, we are actually becoming aware of the more subtle energetic vibrations of the initiating intention. If this is indeed the case, we do not perceive the outcome of the intention in a 'future' point of spacetime, but the not yet physicalized template of our individual and collective intentionality as it flows towards the Now of the present.

It is important to appreciate here that it is not only our conscious mind but also other levels of our awareness that are engendering attention and intention and therefore crystallizing the future.

This has significant implications for our understanding of destiny and free will.

Destiny and Free Will

Science struggles with the concepts of destiny and free will. For the implication that spacetime exists all at once seems to offer only one interpretation: that free will is illusory and that we are essentially automatons who can only play out our destiny. Writings of every ancient tradition, too, have emphasized the power of destiny and our inability to avoid it. Yet as we make choices, it seems that we do so from free will

– although when I see a plate of chocolate biscuits my own free will seems to be absent!

How can this paradox be resolved?

Together the holographic model of the universe and the primacy of integrated consciousness may offer us a means not only of reconciling science and Spirit but also this age-old paradox between destiny and free will.

As we shall go on to explore in coming chapters, our individuated consciousness is vastly greater than the limited awareness of our ego-self. And in this integrative view of ourselves, we make choices on many different levels of perception. So, many of the experiences of our ego-self may indeed be destined, having been chosen by free will at other levels of our awareness. Yet other experiences are the implications of the free-will choices made by our ego-self perception.

This is in accordance with spiritual traditions that have long maintained that at a soul level we choose the circumstances of our birth and life in order to experience and learn from life's lessons. Such intention and choice are then clearly not at the level of our ego-self awareness but at a higher level of our consciousness.

Higher Choices

In beginning to appreciate this – and to recognize that all such choices are ultimately ours – we are empowered to take another great leap forward in our journey of discovery of who we really are.

Recognizing that the implications of our higher choices are in essence our destiny, we can then choose at the level of our ego-self to be in alignment and harmony with them and the greater flow of the Cosmos – or not.

The ongoing challenge for each and every one of us is that our higher-self does not have to physically, mentally or emotionally undergo the challenges and traumas to which it has essentially committed us. We can berate this and rail against the circumstances of our lives, or we can choose to real-ize that our ego-self and higher-self – and indeed all levels of our individuated consciousness – form our soul, and that ultimately, everything we undergo is for the highest good of our soul's evolution.

There is an old adage, 'Before enlightenment carry water, chop wood; after enlightenment carry water, chop wood.' In other words, after recognizing the greater truths and perception that enlightenment brings, we don't necessarily find the circumstances of our chosen lives changing. Our attitude and awareness, however, are transformed.

In our continuing journey throughout *The 8th Chakra* we will still carry water and chop wood, but as fellow travellers we'll learn how to be in ever-greater harmony with the Cosmos, rather than attempting to dam up or divert its flow.

Cosmic Flow

Cosmic flow comprises waves of experience on which we can choose to be cosmic surfers – or not.

I remember once on the island of Maui gazing out over the ocean and seeing some windsurfers ride the Pacific waves like dragonflies skimming over a lake. Watching entranced, I could sense their exhilaration and freedom as they rode perfectly balanced between sea and sky. Present in every moment, I could feel their communion as each wave rose, crested and fell away.

In these significant times, we are all surfers, individually and collectively riding a tidal wave of change. Like those windsurfers of Maui, we can choose to be flexible and responsive to the nuances of the waves of our personal life and those of the great wave we all ride by consciously being in harmony with the circumstances and timing of events.

Alternatively, we can choose to pretend the waves don't exist or have no relevance to us.

But they do and they have.

There is one aspect of the timing of events which offers us a sure sign that we are indeed in the cosmic flow: synchronicity.

The psychologist Carl Jung coined this term to mean a conjunction of events which have no apparent cause but are meaningful to those experiencing them. Jung himself experienced such a synchronicity when treating a patient who at a critical point in her treatment had a dream in which she was given a golden scarab beetle. At her next session, just as she was relating her dream, Jung heard a tapping on the window behind him. On turning round and opening the window, he caught a scarabaeid beetle as it flew, contrary to its normal habits, into the darkened room.

Until then, Jung's treatment had been effectively blocked by his patient's unwillingness to change her rational perspective on life. The scarab, which to the ancient Egyptians was a symbol of rebirth, offered both Jung and his patient transformational insight.

By being open to the possibility of such synchronicities, we welcome deeper magic and higher truth into our lives.

Expect miracles!

Eight Cosmic Principles

There is an octave, an eight-fold group of principles, which, in its various expressions, throughout history and across all cultures, has formed the basis of universal wisdom. Together these principles may be perceived as guiding the co-creativity of all experience. They are the fundamental harmonies by which consciousness expresses itself.

The influence of these principles harmonically resonates not only on the physical plane but also throughout mental, emotional and spiritual realms. They are thus not merely universal but cosmic in nature.

In understanding these cosmic principles we become aware of the underlying means by which consciousness explores itself. And in doing so, we see how the Cosmos in its entirety is ultimately co-created.

Relativity

The first principle of the cosmic octave is the ***principle of relativity*** – real-ativity, probably best represented in the ancient Chinese attributes of yin and yang. These juxtapositions pervade the Cosmos. Inherent within each is the seed of its partner, and in their meeting and balance the third and crucial aspect of creation finds expression.

Take a few moments to discover for yourself the underlying three-fold nature of the universe and this cosmic principle of real-ativity.

- On a sheet of paper draw three vertical columns and, taking just one minute, make a list in the first column of any attributes of the physical world that come to your mind.

- Now in the last column write the opposite of each attribute. For example, if in the first column you have written 'white', write its opposite, 'black', in the end column.

- Finally, take a breath and in the central column write whatever word comes to mind to describe the resolution or balance between the two opposites. For example if you have written 'day' and 'night', you might choose 'dawn' or 'dusk' to express their balance.

I would be extremely surprised if at the end of this little exercise you haven't found a point of balance or resolution between every single pair of opposites on the page.

'Duality' is a word that has been in common usage to describe such juxtapositions of opposites. But the essence of duality is that such opposites are viewed as being separate and each stands alone.

Another word for such opposition is 'polarity'. Whilst originally the term was used to describe the north and south poles of a magnet, its usage has extended to describe the fundamental sundering of consciousness into the myriad forms of yin and yang attributes throughout the world.

If 'duality' describes two strangers standing side by side without touching, 'polarity' encourages them to at least hold hands. Yet there is still a sense that, like the two poles of a magnet, whilst such polarities can balance each other, they can never meet.

However, by describing their interplay as expressing their inherent relationship – or relativity – rather than 'polarity' or 'duality', we can perceive the innate dance between them. And it is through their real-ativity – and its ultimate balance and resolution – that the world is real-ized and we are re-souled.

Resolution

As we shall discuss further in later chapters, when we incarnate in physical form as a man or woman, we embody *both* male (yang) and female (yin) aspects on emotional, mental and higher levels of vibration. Their relationship forms a crucial aspect of our journey to wholeness.

The ancient sages realized that all opposites could ultimately be resolved. They saw the creativity of their communion as embodied in the birth of a physical, metaphorical or symbolic 'child'. This 'child' expression of the trinity, however, is not the energetic offspring of the 'male' and 'female'. It is not later or lesser, but equal to them and is an intrinsic aspect of wholeness.

Reconciliation

The triangle, its three sides culminating at three points or apices, is the simplest geometric form expressing such triadic reconciliation. As architects have long known, it is the most stable of two-dimensional physical forms.

Ultimately, energetic resolutions on all scales of the holographic universe require all three partners – male, female and child – to be equal in the empowerment of their complementary expression, just as the most stable triangle of all is one with three equal sides.

And personally, I wouldn't wish to sit on a three-legged stool where the legs were unequal!

Trinities

This perception of tripartite wholeness reveals itself not only in geometric form but also throughout the myths and symbols that were the preferred teaching methods of the ancients.

The healing symbol known as the caduceus, found in various forms throughout the ancient world, shows two serpents intertwining around a central staff. This represents the interplay and balance of the energetic polarities and the wholeness of their resolution.

In the Vedic pantheon, Brahma the Creator, Vishnu the Preserver and Shiva the Destroyer represent the eternal cosmic cycles of birth, life and death. Such cycles, ever the same and yet ever changing, play themselves out in space and time. And within the same tradition, the three cosmic principles of manifestation, or *gunas*, continually express themselves in an ever-creative dance.

Such fundamental wholeness is also embodied in the almost universal presence of trinities of male, female and child archetypes in ancient cosmologies. To the Egyptians, the mythic Osiris, Isis and Horus embodied these principles. For the Greeks, the relationship of Aphrodite, the goddess of love, and Ares, the god of war, brought forth the child Harmonia, who mediated and resolved their innate conflict. And until deemed heretical by the Church, the Gnostic Christian tradition perceived the cosmic trinity of male Father, female Holy Spirit and androgynous Son – the embodiment of christed awareness.

Triads

Throughout the physical world, the tripartite nature of the whole is continually revealed. It is within the confines of three spatial dimensions that the physical world is manifest.

And embedded within the physical laws that regulate the forces of the universe, these three-in-one themes of mediation, manifestation and resolution are also repeatedly expressed.

In Einstein's famous equation $E=mc^2$, energy and matter, which together form the embodiment of the physical world, are reconciled through the mediation of the speed of light. There is also another way of perceiving this fundamental relationship, thanks to my friend Jeb Barton. I suspect that Einstein would appreciate Jeb's interpretation: enlightenment (E) equals the manifestation (m) of consciousness (c) exploring itself.

Atoms are inherently stable due to the three-in-one balance of the masses, forces and charges of the proton, neutron and electron of which they are comprised. Indeed, the proton is so stable that scientists have estimated that for one to decay into something else would take at least 100 million trillion trillion years!

Subatomic physicists seeking the most elemental structure of Nature have also discovered that just three families of fundamental particles make up all the matter of the universe. And there are also three laws of physical motion which, as Isaac Newton discovered in the 17th century, completely describe movement in three-dimensional space and which are applicable throughout the physical world.

Waves

The waves of energy that are the universal expression of consciousness themselves embody this fundamental three-in-oneness. Each wave begins as an upsurge that then peaks and finally falls away. The vast interaction of waves on all scales of existence then forms the holographic pattern of the Cosmos.

Our experiences are also essentially waves of the expression of consciousness and as such embody tripartite phases. The initiatory journeys that have been the means of gaining wisdom in all cultures at all times inevitably involve three stages. When the 'I' of the initiate is deemed ready they *instigate* the mission or quest. Undergoing the quest forms the *inner-tuition* of the learning process itself. And the third and perhaps most important aspect of the initiation then is the *integration* of the wisdom acquired through endurance and courage.

The fundamental nature of three-in-one resolution pervades our entire way of perceiving the world. We delineate events as being in the past, present or future, good stories need to have a beginning, a middle and end, and we see ourselves as fundamentally embodying heart, mind and will.

Resolution

We have already introduced the second cosmic principle. For as we explore the light and shadow of our experiences, the ultimate aspiration of our integrated consciousness – whether or not our conscious mind is aware of it – is to attain their balance and resolution, or re-soul-ution. Throughout all dimensions and realms of the Cosmos, the **principle of resolution** describes how the energies of consciousness ultimately seek to come into such reconciliation.

The essence of polarity awareness is that each polar element can only be perceived in relation to its partner. Thus we are only aware of light when we have darkness to compare it with. Each needs the other to express itself. By itself, each is also inherently unbalanced. We may judge one polarity as 'bad' and its partner as 'good'. But essentially, the more extreme the manifestation of either, the more unbalanced it is. And in extremis, whatever form the polarity takes, it will become its nemesis. Extreme light will flip into extreme dark and vice versa.

As we continue to judge such polarities, we offer them energy and attention – and inevitably, what we resist persists. The Buddha perceived this cosmic principle when he exhorted his followers to take the middle, Noble path to self-realization and enlightenment.

Ponder this cosmic principle next time you run the hot and cold water together for a bath. Neither is 'good' or 'bad' and their resolution – or re-soul-ution – offers one of our most blissful experiences, especially when combined with bubbles and a glass of wine.

Re-membering

As we explore our polarity-based awareness on the physical plane, we are participants in circumstances. We not only forget that we are spiritual beings having a physical experience but we enter so deeply into our role that the traumas we experience on physical, emotional and mental levels may dis-member our psyche. The inner path to re-membering is then a path of profound healing at the level of our soul. This is the path that we will walk together for the remainder of *The 8th Chakra*.

Our re-membering will involve a process of expanding our awareness beyond the level of our personality and ego-self, for it is within our egoic energy field that the residual imprints of the traumas of our dis-memberment are held. And since, as Einstein pointed out, a problem cannot be solved from the same place that created it, we need to move to a higher vantage point. Ultimately, that vantage point is the awareness of the unity underlying all the diversity of the holographic Cosmos.

This is our journey home to the wholeness of who we *really* are.

Resonance

The ***principle of resonance*** expresses the harmonic correspondences between all things and experiences of the principles and forces of the Cosmos. We discover such correspondences not only throughout the physical world in all its aspects and on all scales, but throughout metaphysical realms too.

This cosmic insight is perhaps best expressed by the wisdom teachings of ancient Egypt. As we have seen, Thoth, the archetypal wisdom-bringer, declared that the entire world resonated 'as above, so below'. In perceiving the macrocosm expressed through the microcosm, he described the fractal and holographic nature of the Cosmos.

The energies of our own thoughts and feelings resonate on both inner and outer levels. Such resonance finds its correspondence in the state of our health and the circumstances of our life.

All our thoughts, e-motions (energy in motion), words and actions embody energy. However, the frequencies, or vibrational levels, of these energies may be high or low. High-frequency energies inspire and vivify us, whereas low-frequency energies deplete and drain us. Ultimately, the higher the frequency of energy, the greater its power to penetrate and transform. Love embodies the highest frequency of energy throughout the Cosmos, whereas emotions such as hate embody the lowest.

According to the principle of resolution, judging such lower-level energies offers them the energy to persist, whilst focusing our attention and intention on higher-level frequencies offers us the path to wholeness and at-one-ment.

As our awareness expands, inevitably we become more coherent in our energy patterns. In doing so, we become more authentic in expressing the purpose of our soul and embody ever-greater integrity. Then both the resonance and the coherence of the higher vibrations of our intention and attention correspond with the eternal harmony of the Cosmos.

We thus learn progressively how to be a cosmic surfer and master of our highest destiny.

Reflection
The *principle of reflection* describes how the outer circumstances of our lives reflect our inner state and vice versa.

This principle is a consequence of the principle of resonance. Our vibrational level resonates with other people and circumstances that embody the same frequencies and we thus co-create circumstances which reflect those realities.

The more we become aware of the inevitability of this principle, the more we are able to pay attention to our own way of being and thus begin the process of transformation. The principle of reflection therefore offers us the ongoing opportunity to develop self-awareness and move towards inner balance. We cannot escape its presence throughout our lives, for it is invariably there in the outer circumstances of our experiences as individuals, families, societies and civilizations. When we heal the one, we heal the whole.

Change
The waves of energies that express consciousness are in

perpetual motion. The *principle of change* underlies this fundamental reality.

The rhythms of our experiences, their highs and lows, their beginnings, creative unfoldings and completions all provide opportunities for us to gain awareness. Depending on our perspective, the continual co-creation of change offers us challenges or opportunities – often in the same moment. But whilst we can try to run from change, we definitely can't hide!

For many of us, the past is our comfort blanket – and some of us cling to it despite it being pretty threadbare. Although being willing to let go sometimes requires a leap of faith and trust in the future, it may offer us the miracle of a rebirth.

I know this in my own life. For some years ago I emotionally attempted to hold on to a marriage that no longer supported either my then husband or me. For months I desperately tried to hang on when I knew in my heart I needed to move on. The emotional anguish became so great that it felt like an iron band crushing my chest every moment of every day.

Early one morning I cried out in despair to Spirit and finally let go of my burden. As I did, within moments I was pain-free. Within days, my husband and I separated and now, nearly eight years on, I am happily remarried and my ex-husband and I remain the soul friends we have been and always will be.

Cause and Effect

The *principle of cause and effect* is the wider metaphysical context of the physical law that every action produces an equal and opposite reaction.

Just as physical laws are fundamentally interconnected, so is the cosmic octave of these eight principles. The principle of cause and effect interweaves with the principle of resolution so that within the experiences of integrated consciousness, such action-reaction processes are ultimately equalized.

Both the principles of change and of cause and effect are embodied in the ancient Vedic concept of karma. Today karma is sometimes misconceived as being the reflection of personal morality or judgement by others or by higher consciousness of our actions. But beyond the limitations of our ego-based awareness, our soul understands the deeper truth of karmic balance and resolution, for the principle of cause and effect embodies, without judgement, the implications of our choices. These, as we have seen, may be made at different levels of our integrated consciousness. And karma is the inevitable process of their playing out – not on the narrow tit-for-tat basis perceived by our ego-self, but in much more profound ways that we may be unaware of unless we expand our awareness beyond the narrow confines of the ego.

As our awareness expands, however, not only do we become profoundly perceptive of the wholeness of the Cosmos, but we naturally align our choices to its ultimate unity. As we do so, the energies of the implications of our choices become balanced and karma is resolved and released.

Conservation

As we know, the waves of energies that are the expression of consciousness are in continual flow. However, whilst the form that the energies take may change, according to the *principle of conservation*, they are ultimately conserved.

This cosmic principle requires us to both give and receive and thereby to allow the ebb and flow of the waves of life to pass harmoniously through us.

We can gain a sense of this profound truth by taking a few breaths.

To begin, take a deep in-breath followed by a shallow out-breath. Then reverse the process and take a shallow in-breath followed by a deep out-breath.

Actually, I should have said, '*Try to…*', for the imbalance between those in- and out-breaths makes it virtually impossible to do.

So now, take a deep in-breath, hold it and, after pausing for a few moments, allow your out-breath to be equally deep and balanced.

I hope you feel better!

Concession

The eighth cosmic principle, which completes the octave of the expression of consciousness, is the **principle of concession**.

Linked to the principle of cause and effect, this describes how once an intention has been set and the choice manifested, concession of its implications is an intrinsic part of the learning and integration of the experience and the development of greater awareness.

Essentially, this principle requires us to acknowledge our responsibility for the circumstances of our lives whilst fully recognizing that our choices may have been made at higher levels of our awareness than our ego-self.

Two other words that are sometimes used here are 'acceptance' and 'allowance'. But when I've explored the nuances between the two descriptions with participants in my workshops, most have felt that 'acceptance' implies a level of resentment – of having to put up with the consequences of causes. 'Allowance' feels more positive and freeing and thus empowers us to take greater responsibility for our life path. However, 'concession' means to acknowledge the truth of something. So when we concede the implications of our choices, we can recognize what then unfolds as being authentic and appropriate.

Cosmic Principles

We've now explored how the coherence of consciousness co-creates actualized states from the quantum field of potentialities. And we've seen how our integral mind makes choices which, according to our perspective, we can interpret as destiny or free will, but which at the highest level are the intention of our soul.

We've also seen how the wisdom of all ages can be distilled into an octave of eight cosmic principles that reveal how cosmic mind guides the experiences of polarity-based awareness.

By perceiving and aligning with these principles of relativity, resolution, resonance, reflection, change, cause and effect, conservation and concession, we can understand what our own higher awareness is seeking to tell us: 'You are consciousness!'

Throughout the following chapters we'll sometimes refer explicitly to one or more of these principles of cosmic wisdom. But even when not overtly expressed, we need to remember that they underlie and guide our every thought, word and action.

And as we walk our path to wholeness, their precepts continually support and guide our steps.

PART II

Feel

CHAPTER 5

Embody Cosmic Harmony

To the Vedic sages of ancient India, the human soul is a droplet of the infinite ocean of consciousness that is *Brahman*. This spiritual metaphor, now many millennia old, sees the journey of the soul reflected in the cycles of life-giving water on Earth. Distilled from the vastness of the cosmic ocean, we soar. Light beings of vapour, we are carried by light breezes and tossed about in the midst of storm clouds until we reach land. Falling as rain, we find our way through the fertile soils of the welcoming Earth and dance within the intricate networks of subterranean water. Aeons may pass before we stream to the surface and then flow with the small and great rivers of life until we find our way back to the ocean.

This ancient metaphor offers us a profound insight into how our individuated consciousness expresses itself. For just as a river is comprised of many tributaries, so our consciousness is far greater than the small stream of the ego-persona we explore in a single human life.

Life After Death After Life

Vedic literature offers us the oldest written teachings of our human family. Their wisdom informed the ancient Chinese, Egyptians and Sumerians and thus many later traditions, all of which perceived the continuation of the human psyche after the demise of the physical body.

Most traditions consider that when we return to Spirit, we move on unless there is a reason for us to remain close to the physical plane. These reasons may include a traumatic demise, when we may not even be aware that we have passed over, or an emotional attachment to a person or place. Whilst many of us, like my beloved mother, may choose to remain close to those we love for a short time after we pass over, remaining for much longer ultimately serves neither those for whom we care nor ourselves. Indeed, spirits sometimes become eventually entrapped through such attachment, remaining long after their loved ones themselves have moved on.

In the last few years investigating such entrapped spirits or ghosts has become a more recognized aspect of parapsychological research. Facilitating their release has also become a more common means of spiritual support.

At the University of Arizona, psychologists Gary Schwartz and Linda Russek have spent several years investigating the claims of mediums who are in touch with the spirits of the departed. They and other researchers who are studying a range of phenomena from near death experiences (NDEs) to after death communication (ADC) are progressively coming to the same view: that there is increasingly strong scientific support for the ancient and spiritual view that our human psyche does continue after our physical body has perished.

Most world religions also believe in some form of reincarnation – the view that we live life after life as we continue to explore what it means to be human. The early Gnostic Christians also held this belief although the concept was subsequently deemed heretical.

The research of psychiatrist Ian Stevenson provides us with the best scientific evidence we yet have for reincarnation. Stevenson has studied the cases of young children who have claimed memories of other lives. He has sought both to minimize the danger of 'false' memories and collect details that can be independently verified. So far, he has amassed over 3,000 case studies indicative of reincarnation.

Our Ego-Self

When we incarnate as a human being, a three-fold stream of consciousness weaves within us the underlying fabric of our life.

The first stream represents our genetic inheritance and thus the lineage of the family and culture we are born into. Whilst the sequence of genes encoded in our parents' DNA is the primary directive for our physical make-up, scientists are also now becoming aware that generational characteristics and environmental factors affecting our parents and even our grandparents can result in the way genes are epigenetically expressed in their offspring.

The second stream is represented by our personality, the emotional and mental lens through which we respond to the circumstances of our experience.

Within the ever-changing matrix of consciousness we call our Solar – or Soular – System, the combined holographic influences of the Sun, Moon and planets at the time and place of our birth engenders the fundamental characteristics of our personality. And these co-ordinates are unique to every one of us, for even identical twins born in the same bed will come into the world a few minutes apart.

The third stream of consciousness arises at the level of awareness of our higher-self. As the purpose for our incarnation or destiny is chosen, so the opportunities and objectives of our life experiences are decided. And it is this level of intention that determines the circumstances of our coming into the world – where and when we are born and who will be our parents – and the subsequent environment in which we live our life.

The dynamic interplay of all three streams is then expressed throughout our life at the level of awareness we call the 'ego-self'.

Mind, Heart and Will

The role played by the awareness of the ego-mind of our 'normal' waking consciousness is primarily to persuade us by all means available to it that its reality – the physical world – is the *only* reality. Furthermore, fulfilling its role of individualizing our experience, it seeks to convince us that we are separate from others and the wider world.

But whilst our ego-mind thus aims to maximize the creativity of our unique perception, our hearts yearn to re-member the unity that underlies the diversity of the holographic Cosmos.

Both mind and heart find their creative expression through our will. The three together form the fundamental trinity of male, female and child principles through which we live life.

We each choose to incarnate either as a man or a woman. Whilst equal, these are intrinsically and energetically different, not just physically but also emotionally and mentally. The inner balance of our male, female and child energies and their appropriate use, regardless of our gender, are fundamental to the full expression of our humanity and a prerequisite for our continuing journey to wholeness.

Subtle Energy Meridians

Vedic wisdom perceives that the subtle energies of the human personality interface with the physical body through the spinning vortices of subtle energies known as chakras.

The chakras are considered to connect with a triad of subtle energy meridians, or *nadis*, known individually as the *pingala, ida* and *shushumna*, which act as conduits for the subtle life-force energies of our biofield.

The trinity of nadis embody our inherent expression of male/yang (*pingala*), female/yin (*ida*) and child/neutral (*shushumna*) energies. These positive/active, negative/passive and neutral/creative principles are depicted by the ancient symbol of healing known as the caduceus. The central staff represents the *shushumna*, up and around which twin serpents representing the *pingala* and *ida* energies coil and come together at each chakra.

As the caduceus reveals, it is the balanced expression of all three cosmic principles within us, as mediated through the chakras, that enables us to manifest the full ego-self.

Chakras

There are seven primary chakras relating to our ego persona. These are located just in front of our spine and extend from our tailbone up to the crown of our head. These are the root chakra (tailbone), the sacral chakra (pelvic area), the solar plexus chakra, the heart chakra, the throat chakra (all located where their names suggest), the third eye chakra (at the centre of the brow just above the base of the nose) and the crown chakra (at the top of the head). These locations have been correlated with the major glands of our endocrine system. Secreting a wide range of hormones whose inter-relationships are not yet well understood, these glands regulate a huge range of physical and emotional responses.

The chakras mediate the subtle energies of our biofield and the freedom with which both subtle and physical energies flow through us is directly correlated to our overall well-being. Any blockages or restrictions will result in imbalance and dis-ease at psychological, emotional or physical levels.

By understanding our chakra system and how it operates, we can become aware of our own energetic blockages. As we do so, we empower ourselves to go beyond the manifestation of dis-ease to its causation and therefore to initiate real and sustained healing.

A Corporate 'Office'

Each of the chakras is traditionally understood to express a different aspect of the human experience. In total, they may be likened to seven floors of a corporate office building.

On the ground floor, the engineering department (root chakra) ensures that all the utilities and facilities that support the corporation's activities are well grounded and have strong foundations.

On the next floor (sacral chakra), the role of the personnel department is to facilitate the appropriate care of everyone in the organization.

The third floor (solar plexus chakra) is dedicated to operational efficiency by ensuring that every activity throughout the corporation works together to express the corporate purpose and creativity.

On the fourth floor (heart chakra) the responsibility of stakeholder services is to make sure that the relationships with all the stakeholders of the organization are met and honoured.

The sales and marketing departments are based on the fifth floor (throat chakra). Their roles are to enable the voice of the corporation to be heard and thus its unique products to be known by and shared with the wider world.

The sixth floor (third eye chakra) is home to the strategic planning team. Here an inner vision is created which allies the organization's resources and capabilities with a wise perception of the outer world to secure and sustain abundance.

On the seventh floor (crown chakra) is the boardroom, where the corporation's disparate activities are brought together and an overview of its well-being and relationships with the wider world is maintained.

Organization to Organism

Just as, in the corporate example, where the focus of the lower three floors is primarily internal to the organization, so the focus of our lower three chakras is ourselves. These three chakras emphasize the basic physical, emotional and security-related needs of our own organism and essentially how we can survive in the world.

The fourth floor, or heart chakra, is where we begin to open up to and empathize with the wider world. And the fifth is where we start to express the unique product that we have to offer – ourselves.

As we ascend through our imaginary corporate office building, we can look out of the window on each floor and get a better view of the surrounding landscape. Similarly, as we ascend through the chakras, our own body gains an expanded view of the wider world.

By the sixth floor, or third eye chakra, we are able to collate our understanding of where we are with the perception of how to go forward in alignment with our resources and higher purpose.

From the vantage point of the seventh floor, the directors have an overall understanding of the entire corporation and its interactions with the world at large. Equally, from the awareness of the crown chakra we gain an overview of our ego-selves and how we relate to others.

Depending on our level of awareness as expressed through each chakra, from the root to the crown, we will interpret differently what are objectively the same outer circumstances or events.

Complementary Energies

Before we go on to discuss each chakra in turn, we need to recognize that in choosing to incarnate as a man or a woman, we are also choosing to manifest the energies of our chakras differently.

Men and women are energetically polarized in a complementary but opposite way, although we all embody the universal principles that we describe as male, female and child. A man primarily embodies the male or yang expression that is energetically directed outward and is active and explosive. Conversely, a woman generally embodies the female or yin expression that is energetically directed inward and is passive and implosive. Crucially, each gender also embodies the child expression which is energetically neutral but from which all creativity arises.

As we move up the body, each chakra also switches its polarity. So for men, the root, solar plexus, throat and crown chakras are expressed in a yang or outward way and the sacral, heart and third eye are expressed in a yin or inward way. For women, the root, solar plexus, throat and crown chakras are expressed in a yin way and the sacral, heart and third eye in a yang way.

Thus men generally express themselves in an outward or yang way through the security needs associated with their root chakra, the urge to express power and purpose mediated by their solar plexus chakra, the communication of their throat chakra and the intellect of their mind. But the yin polarities of their sacral, heart and third eye chakras mean that their expression of the energies of these chakras is naturally directed inwards.

For women, the opposite is generally the case. With the innate active or yang expression of their sacral, heart and third eye chakras, women are naturally able to express inner feelings, empathy and intuitive insights outwardly. But the yin polarity of their root, solar plexus, throat and crown chakras means that issues relating to security, power, communication and intellect are naturally expressed and focused more inwardly.

For everyone, the ever-present child energies are the creative conduit for the combination of these two complementary polarities of yin and yang. Ultimately, the expansion of our awareness enables us to achieve such balance and dance with its appropriate manifestation – not to attempt to homogenize gender expression but to offer ourselves a much richer symphony of experience and spiritual empowerment.

Imbalance to Balance

We'll now review each chakra in turn to understand its perspective and how its energies are expressed both in imbalanced and balanced forms. As we move up the chakras and fully awaken and balance the energies of each, we take a quantum leap in our awareness of the Cosmos, for each represents a progressively higher note of the energies of our ego consciousness.

Imbalances in the chakras, as we shall see, show up in many different guises – but ultimately all of them are about whether we are expressing ourselves authentically and being true to ourselves. When we are, we are in the flow of life and in harmony with the Cosmos, whatever our outer circumstances. We stand straight, neither leaning forwards in our eagerness to prove who we are nor leaning backwards, afraid to show ourselves and fearful of sharing our unique gifts with the world. On page 247 you'll find a simple exercise to help you understand and clear energy imbalances and blockages in each of the seven chakras.

The first three chakras – root, sacral and solar plexus – are primarily about us as individuals. The root is about 'finding our feet' in life, the sacral is about how we gain pleasure and the solar plexus relates to our manifestation of power, purpose and creativity.

The Root Chakra

The root chakra is located at the base of our tailbone or coccyx. Its awareness is instinctual and its aim is to survive. Its sole responsibility is to itself and the sustaining of its own physical needs of shelter and food.

Within the perspective of our ego-self, this chakra is the root by which we connect with the Earth. Like a tree, if our roots are shallow, the storms of life will uproot us, but if our roots are strong and deep, we are supported and nourished.

To feel balanced on this level, we need to physically be where we *need* to be. Each of us has our own authentic needs and it is important that we differentiate them from our desires. If our real need is to live in rural surroundings, the hubbub of a large city will deplete and drain our energies. But if what we truly need is to live in such an urban setting, whilst every one of us needs a connection with Nature in some way, a rural idyll will not sustain and nurture us.

To ensure that the needs of our root chakra are met requires us to be as truthful as we can be with ourselves. To balance the entirety of our lives as best we can, we may be prepared to compromise to some degree with regard to the specific aspects. But every compromise that denies our authentic needs takes us out of balance with ourselves to some degree.

Facing Our Inner Fears

The choice to be where we know we truly need to be will almost certainly require us to face our inner fears to some degree or other. We may as well address this issue now, because it will continue to arise as we consider each chakra in turn.

Fear is a healthy emotion when it alerts us to danger. However, if it becomes chronic at every appearance of change or uncertainty and thus effectively is a continuing way of being, then it is most definitely not healthy.

As we continue our journey to wholeness, fears will almost certainly come up. And as they do, their concerns need to be understood and appropriately honoured. But we must acknowledge that at some stage our inner journey will inevitably take us into the unknown. At that point, as at any time when such uncertainty may arise, all I would encourage you to do is to hear the voice of your heart. Indeed, the very word 'courage' resonates with the French word for heart – *coeur* – and so when we embody courage it is our heart that spurs us on.

And very soon, we'll be sharing a way of listening to the wisdom of the voice of the 8th chakra of the universal heart and our own highest guidance.

But let's now return to the root chakra.

Cultivating Roots

The root chakra's focus is fully on us and no one else. Therefore unless its needs are met and its energies balanced we'll find that survival issues dominate our experiences. Unless our need for security is satisfied, it is unlikely that we will be able to focus on much else in life. So understanding what makes us feel secure is crucial to balancing the root chakra's energies. This is especially true if it seems to us that we never have enough, despite having sufficient resources to sustain our needs.

Cultivating roots where we need to be and in the ways we need to be and beginning to perceive and appreciate the inter-relationship of all life are other important steps in disengaging from the habitual fears of an imbalanced root chakra. If we are not able to do this, we may find our awareness remaining primarily at the root level, with our prevailing emotion being isolation and our sole focus being on material gain.

The Sacral Chakra

The second, sacral chakra is located in the area of our pelvis and its primary energetic drive is the attainment of pleasure as a basis for our physical relationships with the world.

Balancing the energies of this chakra relates to the development of our personal values and discernment as to what we will or won't do to access pleasure. By enjoying an experience in the moment and allowing its pleasure to flow through us rather than hanging onto it, we are able to avoid the danger that the quest for such experience can become its own pleasure. Otherwise, we may entrap ourselves to the extent that as soon as someone or something is attainable or attained, it ceases to offer us pleasure and our quest goes on. When such an imbalance continues, it is ever-more difficult to find fulfilment and we make ever-greater attempts to satisfy a need that cannot be fulfilled. This is called addiction.

Imbalances at this level may, if not curtailed, lead to needing increasing doses of whatever we are addicted to in order to overcome our feelings of emptiness or dissatisfaction. Such a spiral may involve a deep fear of the loss of our pleasures. In relationships this can engender obsessive behaviour, jealousy and a neediness that is unable to be salved.

Also, when we're energetically imbalanced at this level, we may continually compare ourselves with others and in so doing suffer an ongoing feeling of inadequacy.

The first step to balancing the sacral chakra is to see life as joyfully abundant rather than bereft and scarce. Rather than desiring what we don't have, we need to delight in what we do have. Such contentment is not complacency; by being willing to see the abundance in our life as it is, the cosmic principle of resonance is enabled to attract ever-more abundance to us.

To be balanced, each chakra also requires the balance of the one below it. It's like trying to build a house of cards – the security of the upper levels is dependent on the stability of those below. So for the energies of our sacral chakra to be fully balanced, we must resolve any issues relating to those of our root chakra too.

The Solar Plexus Chakra

The solar plexus chakra is located exactly where its name suggests, at our solar plexus, around the area of our navel. This is the power center of the body and mediates the energies relating to our will, purpose and creativity.

With the energies of this chakra we essentially assert who we are to the wider world. Under-use of this chakra may result in an inability to assert ourselves when appropriate or feelings of guilt when we do so. Alternatively, overuse leads to us seeking to impose our will rather than expressing our innate power.

In asserting who we are in a balanced way, we also need to define our boundaries without deliberately or inadvertently raising barriers against the outside world. Such discernment is essential to our progressive self-mastery.

Empowerment

The fundamental principles and values by which we lead our life are engendered in the three lower chakras and balancing the energy of the solar plexus chakra is crucial to embodying their integrity.

On a primary basis, the lower three chakras relate to security, sex and power. When their energies are balanced within us, they are able to support the increasing awareness of the higher chakras.

Here as ever, we need to remind ourselves that energy leads events and not the other way around. So the first step in resolving imbalances in these and all chakras is our intention to do so.

The focus of our intention and the level of awareness of our purpose as mediated by the solar plexus chakra can result in either ego-based power – what I call 'me-powerment' – or the higher purpose of our em-powerment as embodied in our service to others. Such empowerment enables us to resolve conflict through compassion, change competition into co-operation and transform the limitations of control into the freedom of co-creation.

The Heart Chakra

The fourth chakra is located at the level of our heart. As the central chakra of our personality energy field, poised between Heaven and Earth, it is here that the process of integrating our spiritual awareness and physical experience begins.

Whilst the role of our ego-mind is to express our individuality through apparent separation, the role of our heart is to remind us of our ultimate at-one-ment. That is why when we close our hearts down we are entering into a prison of our own making.

Conversely, by letting down our defences, we enable life to flow through us. Our apparent vulnerability is in actuality our greatest strength as we awaken to the knowing that love is the greatest power in the Cosmos.

A sign to us that our heart is awakened and balanced is our ability to both give and receive freely and joyously. For often, the energy of an awakened heart may nonetheless be imbalanced and we may find that whilst we love to give to others, we find it difficult to receive in return. However, by recognizing that by doing so we deprive others of their joy in giving, we can gracefully acknowledge and accept their gifts of love and so regain balance within ourselves.

'Love' is an oft-misused word. We use it to clothe feelings from lust to compassion. Unless the lower three chakras are balanced, the love we feel in our hearts will be conditional and fundamentally about security, sex or power. Our relationships will be needy and co-dependent, rather than empowered and interdependent.

An interdependently loving relationship has been likened to two trees growing side by side. Neither shading each other from the Sun and rain nor denying each other the nutrients of the Earth, their branches and roots are able to receive the full nourishment of Source, which they are then able to share equally with each other.

To live in the heart also requires us to love someone for who they are rather than who we would like them to be or who we think we can make them into – whether or not that is who they would wish to be. While lovingly supporting their intention and efforts to be who they wish to be, we also need to recognize that it is ultimately *their* journey and not ours – they must walk its path, not us.

Such love is unconditional – neither conditioned by the response of the other person nor judgemental of them. A deep dilemma, however, often faces us as we expand our awareness to such a level. For when we love unconditionally does that mean that we must accept the dysfunctional behaviour of our nearest and dearest? My personal perspective is that it doesn't.

Whatever level of awareness we are at, we inherently resonate at that level. Whilst ultimately we thus attract people and circumstances of the same level as ourselves, our integrated consciousness goes on with its co-creative search for the abundance of experiences. So we will continue to encounter people and situations at all levels of awareness. But as we explore the nature of the next chakra, we will see that by connecting with people and events with an awakened and balanced heart chakra, our loving truth unfailingly serves our own and their highest purposes.

The Throat Chakra

The fifth chakra is located at the throat and we awaken its energies by finding our authentic voice and expressing our creativity in whatever way is uniquely right for us.

The communication of such spiritually based creativity is not limited to our spoken voice but embodies the entirety of our personal means of self-expression. When our throat chakra is awakened and balanced, such creativity is inspirational. It flows through us from our higher-self and is beyond the control of our conscious mind. The key to aligning and harmonizing with it is in essence to lose ourselves in its flow by being wholly present in the Now.

An awakened throat chakra can, however, also be imbalanced if the lower chakra energies remain so. We will then find ourselves expressing our 'truth' inappropriately – in anger, frustration or a variety of other ways that reflect those lower imbalances. But the authenticity of our true voice is always heard when we speak from an awakened and balanced heart. And it is then that whatever we are doing and saying is lovingly true and able to reach others at that level.

The Third Eye Chakra

The awakening of the sixth chakra, the third eye, which is located between and just above the level of our physical eyes, offers us an inner-sight into ourselves and into the Divine.

Mother Teresa, when once asked how she could bring herself to wash the destitute beggars of Calcutta, replied that she saw that they were all 'God with dirty faces'.

The third eye chakra, as its name suggests, offers us the intuition – or inner tuition – of our inner vision.

Again, any imbalances in the energies of our lower chakras will be re-encountered as we awaken our third eye. For then our ego-mind will perceive our emerging insights as merely imagination and its doubts will attempt to pull our awareness back to a materialistic world-view where only the physical is 'real'. Our heart-centered intuition, however, knows better and as we allow ourselves to hear and actively listen to its guidance, it will steer us ever-safely onward.

Conversely, as the third eye chakra continues to awaken, if we ignore the advice of our intuition, we will invariably experience consequences whose severity – and I speak from personal and rueful experience – is in direct relationship to the level of our awakening.

Being pro-active rather than merely reactive with our intuitive sense opens up the magic of synchronicity. When we begin to perceive the interconnected threads of circumstances and events and allow ourselves to be guided by their flow, we dance in harmony with the Divine. We begin to real-ize the real-ity that nothing happens by chance and we become ever more aware that there is an inherent purpose that underlies and guides the flow of life, even though we may not understand its reasoning.

Awakening and balancing the energies of the third eye chakra have been understood for many millennia as a major step on the spiritual path to transcendence. But here I would stress that such awareness is ultimately to enable us to embody the wholeness of who we *really* are through the miracle of human life and not to avoid or escape its circumstances and challenges.

The Crown Chakra

As we awaken the energies of the crown chakra we are able to perceive the universe as an inter-connected conscious whole and ourselves as both a microcosm and the entirety of its holographic nature.

With the balanced opening of our crown chakra, we have arrived at the threshold between being alone and being able to perceive our all-oneness with the Cosmos. When we step over that threshold, we begin to directly experience how the One is expressed through the diversity of the many.

The balanced energies of our crown chakra enable us to discern the world as innately sacred and suffused by divine presence. We also come to know that we truly are a droplet of the cosmic ocean. So how could we not have direct access to our own divinity?

The Alter Major Chakra

Ancient tradition refers to the third eye and crown chakras as offering us inner and outer mental views of the world respectively. But less well known is that high initiates were also able to access the synthesis of these views and thereby realize that our inner and outer perceptions are reflections of each other. Their ability to connect with such transcendental realities was achieved through a further chakra at the base of the skull, termed the *alter major* chakra.

As our individual and collective awareness is expanding,

this chakra is becoming of crucial energetic significance. For by accessing and balancing the energies of the alter major chakra with those of our heart and solar plexus chakras, we are now able to raise our vibration to perceive and activate the 8th chakra of the universal heart.

Embody Cosmic Harmony

The energies and awareness of our lower chakras are about taking responsibility for our conscious choices and their implications. As we awaken the heart and higher chakras, we progressively open up to and align with the awareness of our higher-self.

Our willingness to embody such alignment has been called surrender. And indeed it is, as we let go of our ego-self reliance and let God guide us onwards. But this is not a sacrifice of who we think we are – it is re-membering who we *really* are.

In the next chapter we'll go on to discuss archetypal, transpersonal and collective consciousness and how these higher levels of awareness are fundamental aspects of our psyche.

CHAPTER 6

Breathe Out . . .

We have just explored the nature of our egoic or personality-based self. Let's now take an out-breath into the vast matrix of consciousness to which we have access.

Going beyond the ego-self to experience such expanded states of awareness has been the goal of spiritual seekers from time immemorial. From the mists of prehistory onward we have had the potential to access such states, and mind-altering substances and psycho-spiritual techniques have been way-showers to these realms. But whilst mystics and initiates throughout history have sought these extraordinary states of being, for the great majority of people the mundane realities of ordinary life have prevailed.

No longer.

Individually and collectively, we are now – every one of us – beginning to be able to access higher levels of awareness. And crucially, we are becoming able to do so without recourse to the mind-altering substances and psycho-spiritual means of our forebears.

Equally, over the past two millennia, religious institutions have exercised spiritual authority. Gurus or priests, whether benevolent or malevolent, have been perceived as the privileged conduits of Spirit.

No longer.

In embodying the energies of the 8th chakra, each one of us can now empower our own spirituality and access the wholeness of who we really are.

Whilst we can continue to walk alongside our fellow travellers in whatever spiritual tradition we choose, we are also able to tread the inner path that is ours alone – and yet leads to our common destination.

The Collective Unconscious

From his research into altered states of consciousness, psychologist Carl Jung identified a vast group awareness to which we all have access. He called it the 'collective unconscious' and perceived it to be the archive of our entire cultural and historical heritage.

Jung also identified primeval creative principles he termed 'archetypes', whose essences pervade the collective unconscious and which therefore find expression in both our individual lives and in humanity as a whole.

Such archetypes make up the pantheons of deities the world over. Whilst we may perceive them in ways that are culturally specific, their innate nature is generic and their guidance and presence are common to us all.

As we expand our awareness beyond our ego-self, we access the collective unconscious and the realms of archetypal beings. In doing so, we begin not only to perceive but also to directly experience that the boundaries between our psyche and the Cosmos are essentially arbitrary.

In such states of awareness we are able not only to access knowledge throughout space and time but to experience on a nonlocal basis that journeys beyond the world of manifestation. We may obtain information that appears to be memories of other lives, or we may identify with other beings

– animals, trees, mountains and rivers – and become intimately aware that they too are sentient.

As Jung also discovered, such states are able to offer new and accurate information that cannot be derived by the means hitherto open to our ego-based mind. For example, when the shamanic healers of the Amazon Basin, the greatest repository of medicinal plants on Earth, were asked by researchers how they had gained their encyclopaedic knowledge of the properties of the plants, they replied, 'The plants told us.' Anthropologists, who have for generations brought a materialistic world-view to their research, are now beginning to discover for themselves such metaphysical knowledge by undergoing the same vision quests as the primary peoples whose cultures they are studying.

What is clear from all the accounts of such experiences is that whilst the archetypes themselves are bridges to the ultimate Source of all creation, they are not the Source itself. Mistaking them for the Source has been the historical path to idolatry, division and disempowerment. But understanding them as a real part of an almost infinite holographic consciousness enables all cultural limitations to be transcended and a greater awareness of both the Cosmos and our place within it to be attained.

Ultimately, at the very frontier of human perception, there is a level of awareness that embraces all polarities. Everyone who has directly experienced it acknowledges that it is beyond the power of language to describe – an ineffable field of pure mind, unconditional love and creative power. Sublime music allows us a clearer glimpse of it than words, however poetic. The sight of Nature in her full glory gifts us another. But the language that resonates at ever-higher levels of awareness is that of love – not the words that seek to describe love, but the inner feelings that leave no doubt as to its reality. And not the feelings that seek to judge or condition love, but the feelings that set it free.

As our awareness continues to expand, we may choose to merge into this consciousness, to witness it in blissful awe or to embrace it as the Beloved of our heart, mind and will.

Shamans, Geomancers and Mystics

The world over, metaphysical traditions have understood that our feelings, thoughts and sensory awareness are mediated through the three centers of our mind, heart and will. In turn these have been correlated with the archetypal gender associations of male, female and child.

Different cultures at different times have emphasized these three different aspects of our human experience in seeking to explain the world and our purpose on Earth. To scientists and geomancers, both ancient and modern, the way of the mind has opened up a vast storehouse of cosmic knowledge. Over the last three centuries, we have collectively walked this path and in doing so have delved further into the mysteries of the physical world than ever before. But because the role of the mind is to individualize our perception, the price we have paid for such outer sight has been the progressive blindness of our inner-sight.

To indigenous shamans, the path to understanding is the heart-centered way of direct experience and the innate feeling of being a thread in a vast web of life. For followers of this path, the entire Cosmos is alive and all life is honoured and perceived through relationship. This is the way of deep ecology, of walking lightly upon the Earth and of co-operating with, rather than fighting, cosmic cycles.

The third way, the way of the will, has been trodden by the mystics of many traditions, for whom intuitive revelations replete with miracles have formed the path to glimpsing the creative purpose of the Cosmos.

These three paths have the same ultimate destination and are not mutually exclusive. Indeed, the integration of our mind, heart and will is essential to accessing the portal of the 8th chakra and continuing our journey to wholeness.

Archetypal Numbers

Many wisdom traditions teach that the wholeness of the human soul is embodied by a matrix of consciousness comprising an integrated 12-into-13 harmonic of fundamental energies. Such teachings rely on the use of symbol and metaphor to depict this understanding. And so throughout the archetypal language of myth, in the journey of the solar – or soular – hero, the inner pilgrimage to wholeness, we repeatedly encounter these archetypal numbers. Twelve companion deities surrounded Osiris, the ancient Egyptian god of regeneration. Twelve followers accompanied the archetypal hero Odysseus, whose long journey home after the Trojan War was recounted by Homer. Hercules the Greek hero undertook 12 labours to complete his mission and attain freedom. And Jesus, whose birth we celebrate at the winter solstice – the rebirth of the Sun – had 12 disciples.

This interweaving of 12 around one is reflected in the astronomical and astrological cycles of the zodiac and the cosmic dance of the Sun, Moon and Earth. Each year the Sun completes a cycle against the background of the 12 constellations of the zodiac. And each year the Moon, as it circles the Earth, traces out 12 sidereal months as measured against the stellar background and 13 full Moons or lunations.

The same harmonic is embedded within the musical notes of the chromatic scale, where, as we have seen, the 13th note both completes an octave – by doubling the frequency of the first note – and begins the next. To the initiated musicians of ancient Greece the innate geometrical relationships embodied by the chromatic scale reflected cosmic principles of evolution and the embodiment of unity consciousness.

The ancient geometers depicted Spirit as a perfect sphere. To them the embodiment of Spirit in matter was further revealed by the greatest number of spheres able to be packed around a central sphere of the same size, being 12 around one.

It was these intuitive insights which reconciled so many ancient cultures in a common perception.

Ordinary and Extraordinary

The journey of re-membrance takes us to levels of awareness far beyond the illusory constraints of our personal self. The attainment of such states has generally been perceived as the culmination of a lifetime of devout dedication and hitherto been viewed as only available to those who would renounce the everyday world. Indeed, for many spiritual traditions, the physical world, by its very nature, has been seen as being 'fallen' and 'sinful' and such traditions have considered that only by removing themselves from the 'temptations' of that world could seekers discover their higher spiritual selves.

Whilst understanding the thinking from which such views derive, I personally feel that at this time our highest purpose in being here in physical incarnation is to embody the spiritual wholeness of who we really are through our human experience. Some years ago, on a beautiful morning as I walked in Avebury's sacred landscape, I received the following clairaudient message:

In the commonality of our humanity, we are all ordinary.
In the commonality of our divinity, we are all extraordinary.

I realized then that we are here to express our cosmic nature
in all its ordinary and extraordinary splendour – to embody
the divine in the mundane and to see that divinity is the
natural way of the world.

The Tides of History
Over the aeons of time that have unfolded since the
beginning of the universe, the evolution of complexity has
enabled ever-greater levels of awareness to be individually
and collectively experienced on the physical plane. And
during the cosmic blink of time which represents the
collective human story, we have continually sought deeper
understanding of our place in the Cosmos and communion
with its higher realities.

Like the great tides of the ocean, pulled to and fro in thrall
to the Moon, the tides of human history have ebbed and
flowed. And we are all surfers on the waves that are the
circumstances of our individual and collective lives as they
rise, peak and fall away. We each have our destined role in
their interplay of light and shadow and we are all here now at
this momentous time to play our part in what has been called
by many mystics a Shift of Ages.

Stretched to Breaking Point
We now know that evolution is characterized by slow
trends interspersed with revolutionary leaps. Approximately
50,000 years ago, fully modern humans first appeared in
the fossil record. Since then, whilst our cognitive abilities

have hardly changed at all, we have individually and collectively explored the full gamut of polarity-based awareness.

For the first 40,000 years of the journey of our species, the available evidence indicates that we understood that we were spiritual beings undergoing a physical experience and embraced a shamanic world-view like those of contemporary hunter-gatherers. Shamanic communities see themselves as part of a great web of life within whose cycles of birth-life-death and rebirth they tread lightly on the living Earth, in harmony with their fellow creatures.

But over the last ten millennia, new world-views arose that were characterized by a different relationship with the Earth and the wider Cosmos. With the advent of farming and the domestication of animals, our relationship with the natural world underwent a revolution. No longer was humanity at the mercy of Nature. Now we began to view the world around us as something we could tame and control. From perceiving ourselves as an intrinsic but not particularly advantaged thread in life's great web, we began to see ourselves as progressively gaining dominion over that web. And from seeing the Earth as intrinsically sacred, we began to perceive ourselves as being at the centre of the Cosmos.

Over the centuries, the different cultures that sought ever-greater domination over the Earth and her children compromised and eventually destroyed our intimacy with both her and the Cosmos. As we explored our separation and newly discovered individuality, we began to feel and even revel in the perception that we were alone. But as the schism grew ever larger we began to feel lonely.

For the last 300 years, materialistic science has sought to convince us that the physical world is without purpose and that it is the only reality. In its most fundamentalist form, science has also maintained that we are solely the random outcome of evolutionary processes where the only motivation is survival. Thus our collective exploration of polarity perception has, like an elastic band, been stretched to breaking point.

Danger and Opportunity

The Chinese symbol for 'crisis' juxtaposes the glyphs for 'danger' and 'opportunity'. And in the perfect cosmic timing of this moment, as we appear to stand on the edge of an abyss, we are also expanding our awareness to gain the understanding of how we may leap the chasm that lies before us.

Until now, to explore the fullness of polarity-based perception we have, like all actors, needed to convince ourselves of the reality of the play we are enacting. Now, however, for the first time in human history, we are personally and collectively able to balance and transcend the limitations of polarity-based awareness. We are now able to embody unity consciousness, as did the avatars who have been our spiritual way-showers over the ages. And we are able to do so without giving away our personal empowerment to any intermediary.

As spiritual beings undergoing a physical experience, we are ready to undertake a greater challenge and to embrace a greater opportunity. At last we are able to embody the energies and awareness of the 8th chakra and thus complete the fundamental octave of awareness and consciously reclaim the wholeness of our soul.

Transpersonal Chakras

Beyond the seven-fold chakra system of our personality are

five higher transpersonal chakras. At ever-higher vibrational levels of holographic perception they complete the 12-fold energy field and attain the 13th whole of the awareness of unity consciousness.

The 8th Chakra

The 8th chakra of the universal heart is the bridge between our ego-based perception and our higher awareness. On a collective level, we are now experiencing our resonance with this chakra as an increasingly global compassion. Most people individually feel its presence as an energy centre positioned between the personal heart and throat chakras.

Energetically, the 8th chakra may be perceived as bringing together the trinity energies of our mind, heart and will as expressed through our alter major, heart and solar plexus chakras. In essence the triadic nature of the universal heart thus creates an energetic portal, balancing and raising our awareness to a transpersonal level.

Unconditional love is the vibration of this level of perception and as we reverberate with its essence we gain a new understanding of the archetypal consciousness that guides our human experience.

The 9th Chakra

The 9th chakra is located approximately a hand's length beneath our feet. The energies of this so-called earthstar chakra offer us a much more profound connection with the Earth than does our personal root chakra. By connecting with the Earth through the earthstar chakra, we are able to commune at ever more profound levels with the devic and elemental realms of the living Earth.

The 10th Chakra

The 10th chakra is located energetically about a hand's breadth above our head and connects us with the matrix of the group soul that is the consciousness of our entire Solar – or Soular – System.

Through the experience of these higher chakras, people are beginning to heal the traumas of their soul journeys and to re-member their soul identity at terrestrial, intra-terrestrial and extra-terrestrial levels.

The 11th Chakra

The 11th chakra, approximately 18 inches above the crown of our head, connects us at galactic levels of awareness.

As we expand our perception to incorporate the consciousness of these transpersonal chakras we are able to access the wisdom and guidance of the multi-dimensional realms of the Cosmos and our own highest awareness and intuitive guidance.

At this moment of global crisis, such higher wisdom may indeed offer us the keys to a future in which we are consciously in harmony with the Cosmos and ready to become the master navigators of our individual and collective destinies.

The 12th Chakra

The 12th chakra, which is located 36 inches above our head, connects us with the unity consciousness of the entire Cosmos and offers us the ultimate re-membering of who we *really* are.

For, as the 12 together become the transformational thirteenth, the unity of the One which transcends and gives birth to all relativity consciousness is realized.

Our Soul Purpose

The 8th chakra of the universal heart completes the octave of perception that is our personality-based consciousness and is the portal to our higher transpersonal awareness.

In earlier chapters we've seen the fundamental importance of three-in-one principles and how their combined energies resolve the tensions that are innate in the expression of polarity. Within the consciousness of our ego-self, on an energetic level, our mind, heart and will embody this cosmic trinity. It is through our inner thoughts and feelings and our interactions with the outer world as mediated by our will that we experience what it means to be human.

Also, as we have seen, each of our seven personality-based chakras incorporates male, female and child energies, and these active, passive and neutral (or creative) principles are also termed, respectively, the *pingala, ida* and *shushumna* in the Vedic tradition.

At a higher level of the cosmic hologram, our mind, heart and will also incorporate these three-in-one cosmic principles. For whether we were born a man or a woman, our feelings are essentially female, or passive, and our thoughts male, or active, and our will expressed through the creative energies of the cosmic 'child'.

When these are in balance, the energies of the 8th chakra can be accessed. If, however, either the male or female energies become dominant, their creative expression through the will becomes imbalanced.

Over the last two millennia, our collective psyche has been characterized by the progressive dominance of the mind. And whether or not we are physically male or female, we have collectively denigrated the power of the heart.

I believe that we have extended such energetic imbalance as far as our collective psyche has agreed to do so and the redressing of this imbalance is intrinsic to our opening the portal of the 8th chakra of the universal heart.

In accessing the universal heart, we transcend the limitations of our ego-based awareness and real-ize the multi-dimensional beings we really are. We also begin to comprehend the purpose of our soul.

To do so, we now need to consider how our expanding awareness resonates with the matrices of consciousness, first of the Earth and then of our Solar – or Soular – System. Though the crises of these times embody great risks and dangers, we are also offering ourselves an incredible opportunity to re-establish our relationship with these innate aspects of the cosmic hologram.

CHAPTER 7

The Living Earth

The Earth is a living being. She is not a passive backdrop to our lives. Nor is she an enemy to be subdued and overcome. Nor is she a replaceable product to be abused and abandoned. Yet we treat her with such ignorance, aggression and disdain. Despite all this, she continues to nurture us – but for how much longer?

Not only is the Earth the only home we have, she is the only home available to us for the foreseeable future. And as we shall see, she is our evolutionary partner in the Shift of consciousness that is now imminent.

Some of us speak of 'saving the planet', whilst others ignore or are oblivious to such pleas. The reality is that it is not the Earth who needs saving; it is us. For ultimately she will survive whatever puny abuse we shower upon her and whatever changes she is currently undergoing. We, however, will not.

At an exponential rate, we are poisoning and destroying the environment that has abundantly sustained us for hundreds of millennia. And, like a virus that spreads and destroys its host, we are collectively rushing heedless towards disaster – disaster that is avoidable.

The immense resources spent on so-called defence are no defence against the greatest threat we actually face. If a fraction of the global energy and resources spent on the development and use of weapons were refocused on the development of harmonious technologies and industries in partnership and co-operation with the Earth – and with each other – we might still prevail. But this asks more of us than a change of mind – it also asks for a change of heart and of will. And it requires an expansion of our awareness.

Whilst there is research pioneering such harmonious technologies, it is minuscule compared to the now urgent need. My book *The Wave* discusses such developments and possible environmental solutions in more detail, but here let's consider the consciousness and biofield of Gaia, as the ancient Greeks termed the Spirit of the Earth. For as we do so, we can begin to perceive other ways in which we can reconnect with her, listen to her deep wisdom and learn to live in harmony with her.

From Domination to Stewardship

In seeking domination rather than stewardship of the resources of the living Earth, we have in ignorance and carelessness broken the strands of her Gaia's way of life. And until recently science has brought an overwhelmingly reductionist and materialistic mindset to its understanding of her.

Now, however, as we have seen, science is discovering the holographic nature of the universe at all scales of existence, from the minute strings which form the fundamental 'notes' of energy and matter to complex systems such as weather patterns and earthquakes. Such holographic resonance is also being revealed throughout biological systems, from individual organisms to ecosystems, and its harmonic patterns underlie the entirety of evolution. The ancient perception of the harmonious partnership between the natural environment and biological life is being re-evaluated and progressively understood as being innately co-evolutionary.

The pioneering work of James Lovelock, the first person since the ancient Greeks to call the Earth by the name Gaia, has ushered in a new era of deep ecology and appreciation for her biorhythms. Lovelock was amongst the first to identify the intricate and self-organizing means by which Gaia has been able to sustain biological life for nearly four billion years, despite at least four cataclysms that each destroyed over three-quarters of the life then extant. He has also recognized the consequences of our unconscionable abuse of our planetary home in his new book, *The Revenge of Gaia*.

Honour

We share our ecosystems with the animals and plants that feed and thus sustain us, and yet very few of us honour these fellow beings, let alone acknowledge that they may have feelings. Naturalists, however, are increasingly discovering that they do.

Animals have now been found to experience emotions, including love and the suffering of grief and fear. Indeed, how could they not have individual feelings, at least at some level, when scientists are attempting to identify every human emotion as an evolutionary development?

We have closed our collective eyes to the suffering of animals. Advocates of industrialized farming methods have denied that such methods are cruel. But there is irrefutable proof that they are. How then can we continue to accept such barbarism?

Whilst there are sound ecological and personal health reasons for eating substantially less meat than we do, the choice to eat meat is still an appropriate one. For the last ten millennia we have co-habited with domesticated animals to our mutual benefit. Only in the last half-century or so has our partnership become so prevalently abusive.

It doesn't have to be like this. There are humane methods of breeding, rearing and killing animals for food. Factory farming, however, is an abomination. Not only do the animals suffer but also, as we have seen, such energetic patterns are imprinted on a cellular level. So every animal that is reared in misery and dies in pain is passing on those emotions to everyone who eats their flesh. Consider the effect on human health.

Plant Sentience

In the 1960s researcher Cleve Backster demonstrated that plants were also sentient and responded to pleasure and pain. Backster's experiments showed, however, that the plants were immediately responsive to his thought rather than to his subsequent action. When he merely pretended to harm a plant, there was no reaction at all – the plant appeared able to differentiate between real and pretend intent. Backster was able to detect a reaction even when a leaf was detached from the plant.

The plants also reacted to unformulated threats. Backster discovered that if a plant was threatened with overwhelming danger or damage it 'played dead' by retreating into a deep state of dormancy.

Lie-detector tests carried out by Backster also showed that plants were able to tell truth from lies. Further experiments showed that plants had memory and, once attuned to a particular person, were able to maintain that link even when the person was elsewhere.

Other researchers, such as Marcel Vogel, Randall Fontes and Robert Swanson, have all validated Backster's findings that plants have a level of sentience. And by attaching electrodes to single cells, amoeba, yeast, mould cultures, biofilms, blood and sperm, Backster himself has been able to show that all exhibit reactions akin to those of plants.

Such investigations are in their infancy and improved methodologies and wider-ranging research are needed to verify the claims of the few researchers who are undertaking this work. Nonetheless, the preliminary work that has been done supports the anecdotes of all green-fingered gardeners who have the sensitivity and sense to commune with their plants. Such gardeners also know that by communicating with a plant that is about to be picked or cooked, they can put it at ease and thus obviate any energy of fear.

In the web of life, the roles that many plants take are of inestimable benefit to us. All they seem to ask of us in return is that we honour their gifts and offer gratitude, as do primary peoples worldwide.

The True Price of Food
The re-establishment of a respectful relationship with the animals and plants that share our planetary home is now urgent. The food we eat in the West may look good, but has been found to have only a quarter of the nutritional value of the food of two generations ago. We are eating more than our ancestors and yet suffering from malnutrition. This, together with our lifestyle choices to eat chemically treated and processed food replete with toxins, is ensuring that not only we but also our children are progressively being at best malnourished and at worst poisoned.

The industrial methods perpetrated over the last two generations and the exponential increase in processed foods has led us now to a level of sickness – obesity, allergies, diabetes and heart disease – that is unprecedented.

By not including the ill-health-related costs in the true price of food, we are completely deluding ourselves that our food is cheap. If these ill-health costs were added to the prices for industrially grown and processed food and then compared to the equivalent prices for organic and fresh food, we would see that the latter are actually cheaper.

The market for processed foods has become so huge because we are also busier than our parents and grandparents were and we perceive such foods as 'fast' and convenient. Whilst superficially they are, if we were to add up the time lost through illness and the shortening of our life spans, we would see how blind we have been to the months and years they are actually costing us.

If we want to regain our health, we must immediately reverse this appalling trend, not only for ourselves but also for our children. There is now an entire generation growing up that needs to be re-educated in their eating habits if they are not to have a life expectancy, and indeed quality of life, that is worse than our own.

Our body is the grail through which our consciousness explores the physical world. Our embodiment of the higher levels of awareness that are now available to us requires us to have a concern for our physical well-being. And if we are to fulfil our destiny, we need to seek health and balance of both our inner and outer environments.

The outer environment, too, bears the damaging costs of our industrial methods, not only in food production but throughout virtually all the technologies that have been developed to exploit the resources of Gaia. To understand how we may reconcile and re-establish our relationship with the living Earth, we now need to consider the ninth or earthstar chakra located beneath our feet.

The Earthstar Chakra

In the last chapter we discussed how our consciousness connects with the Earth on a personal level through the root chakra. But as we begin to access the higher awareness of our transpersonal chakras, we need to ground these more powerful energies through the earthstar rather than our root chakra. The reason for this is that, like a tree, the higher our energetic branches reach, the deeper our energetic roots need to be to keep us grounded and secure.

Connecting through the earthstar also helps us to access the consciousness of the living Earth and the wisdom of her multi-dimensional realms, as we will discuss further in the next chapter.

On page 251 there is a universal heart and earthstar meditation to help you connect with, integrate and ground these transpersonal aspects of ourselves.

Electromagnetic Beings

We are all electromagnetic beings who interact not only within ourselves but also with our physical environment primarily through the resonance of electric and magnetic influences.

Our perception of reality is not only dependent on the five-fold sensory input from our surroundings. Certain environmental energies can bypass these senses and resonate directly with the energy systems of the body to create altered states of reality in some cases every bit as 'real' as normal waking consciousness.

For example different low-level magnetic field strengths and frequencies can slow down, switch off or stimulate brain activity. And over-stimulation by low-level electric currents has been associated with visual illusions and hallucinations.

In the early 1980s it was discovered that the magnetic field of Gaia also affects our pineal gland and our internal biological clock. When we are shielded from the Earth's field our circadian rhythms are significantly desynchronized. Indeed, generators providing a low-level magnetic field are now routinely fitted in spacecraft to preserve the natural biorhythms of astronauts during long space flights.

It is not just our brain that is affected. The human body acts as a tuning device resonating powerfully with particular frequencies of electromagnetic radiation. In addition to our brain, the ethnoid sinus, thymus, liver, spleen, heart, lungs and the haem in our blood are particularly sensitive.

Pulsed low-frequency magnetic fields are currently used to treat bone fractures, and magnets are applied to alleviate the symptoms of arthritis and rheumatism. Research and anecdotal evidence are also suggesting that natural radioactivity can cause altered perceptions of time and in small doses may even have beneficial healing effects.

Mainstream medicine now recognizes the diagnostic power of technologies based on electromagnetic fields. The power of x-rays to see inside the body has been utilized for many years. Now, when combined with computer processing, CAT scans enable three-dimensional images of the tissues and organs of the body to be created. MRI scans, which utilize magnetic resonance acting on the hydrogen atoms of the water within our bodies, also create internal images that are incredibly detailed.

New techniques continue to emerge that recognize the power of light and electromagnetic fields to heal by resonating with the body's natural fields and promoting health. For instance, over 60 per cent of the population in the UK are estimated to suffer the pain and disfigurement of cold sores caused by the herpes virus. But by enhancing the body's immune system, a focused beam of infrared light, with no harmful side effects, is now being pioneered to cure the sores in less than half the time of any other remedy.

Schumann Resonance

Gaia, too, is an electromagnetic being replete with multi-frequency energies. Many of these, both within the Earth's crust and throughout the atmosphere, are of very low frequencies that correspond to those of our brainwaves. In other words, at levels below our waking awareness, we are profoundly entrained with the consciousness of Gaia.

In 1952 W.O. Schumann discovered that within the atmosphere and encircling the Earth there is an ongoing harmonic pattern of standing waves creating a continual energy field with a resonant frequency of 7.83 cycles per second. Termed 'Schumann resonance', its fundamental frequency correlates to the mid-range of the alpha rhythms of our brain – the range of frequencies we exhibit when we are in a meditative state. And since Schumann made his discovery, measurements of this innate environmental resonance have also revealed overtones of its basic frequency, all of which lie within the range of human brainwaves.

Magnetic Pole Reversals

Gaia's electromagnetic field is crucial to the biological life she sustains. But how the field arose and how it has persisted for nearly four billion years remains a mystery to science. Whilst geologists know that Gaia's outer core, of molten iron suffused by precious minerals such as platinum and gold, acts as a geo-dynamo, how it does this is as yet unknown.

Periodically, however, the polarity of Gaia's magnetic

field flips. So what is now the magnetic north pole was once the south – and will be again, possibly very soon. Currently the north magnetic pole is over 1,000 miles away from the geographical North Pole. The magnetic north is moving very rapidly – for geological processes – at around 25 miles each year and is currently off the coast of western Greenland. The magnetic field strength has also been reduced at an accelerating rate by some 10 per cent over the last 150 years. Both of these are signs that a pole reversal is imminent – in fact it is way overdue. In the past – the last one was approximately 700,000 years ago – the entire flip only took about 4,000 years.

We do know from the fossil record that such flips don't appear to have a detrimental affect on animals. Indeed, our hominid ancestors were walking the Earth during the last event. But the record is unable to show what the effects on consciousness may have been in the past or may be in the future. Although we don't yet know, it could be that such a magnetic reversal triggers shifts in awareness. And, as we'll see, metaphysicians are predicting that such a shift will occur in the 2012/2013 timeframe.

We should not, however, forget that for our fellow creatures such as migrating birds and whales, the reduction and reversal of their magnetic way-showers might sadly have serious and unavoidable consequences.

Dragon Paths

Just as energy meridians flow through our own body, similar channels also network the energetic body of Gaia. The ancient Chinese called these *lung mei*, or 'dragon paths', and sought to locate their homes so as not to disturb their flow.

In 1921, an English entrepreneur named Alfred Watkins

had a clairvoyant vision where he saw the landscape of his native Herefordshire networked by lines he called 'leys', after ancient clearings in the forests that had covered the land millennia before. He perceived such straight tracks as following ancient pathways and connecting ancient sites.

As interest in such alignment leys increased, dowsers began to sense Earth energies associated with such lines. But unlike Watkins' straight alignments, these energy leys were sinuous and akin to the *lung mei* of the Chinese geomancers, or dragon masters.

Over the last 50 years Western geomancers have also discovered that energetic grids encompass Gaia and that the subtle energies of her biofield are in the form of a dodeca-hedron. This is the fifth of the five elemental solid shapes which the ancient geometers considered to be the idealized templates of physical forms and their interface with Spirit. These five are named 'Platonic solids' after the Greek philosopher Plato. Two-and-a-half millennia ago he was the first to describe their geometrical properties and to ascribe one of the primary elements of Earth, Water, Air and Fire to each. To the fifth, the dodecahedron with its 12 five-sided faces, he ascribed the element of Aether – an all-pervasive universal energy, whose existence is now being re-evaluated by cosmologists.

Plato was also the first to describe the grid of Gaia as a dodecahedron. In the 1970s, three Soviet researchers, Nikolai Goncharov, Vyacheslav Morozov and Valery Makarov, announced their discovery of a grid of Earth energies corresponding to this ancient understanding. In physical terms, the grid equates to electromagnetic stress lines around the globe. To some degree it also correlates to the formation of the tectonic plates on which the continents drift and which allow Gaia to continually recycle and replenish the rocks of her crust and thus sustain the fertility of biological life.

Water

Water comprises approximately two-thirds of the surface of Gaia and also of the human body. It is crucial for life, has extraordinary abilities to carry and transform energies and is able to retain memory.

Since 1994, Japanese scientist Dr Masaru Emoto has studied the innate nature of water and has discovered that it responds both to environmental conditions and to human emotions.

By freezing and then photographing droplets of water from various sources, Emoto has obtained some remarkable and revolutionary images. What he has found is that water from a pristine source such as a mountain stream forms ice crystals of exquisite delicacy and symmetrical geometry. But water obtained from polluted sources has misshapen crystals, contorted from their natural perfection.

Going further, Emoto played a variety of different types of music to samples of pure water, then froze and photographed the droplets. When he observed the frozen images, he saw the implications of how different music energetically affects the water in our own bodies. Whereas the ice crystals of water exposed to classical music or folkloric tunes were found to embody their harmonic symmetry, those exposed to heavy metal and rock music were, like the water from polluted sources, distorted as though in pain.

Emoto's research adds to the growing awareness that as innately resonant beings, we are profoundly affected by the energies of our environment.

Geomancy

Our current Western lifestyles and world-view desensitize

us to whatever natural energies may be prevalent in the environment and even encourage our disparagement of their existence. Yet for millions of years our evolving species was intimately interconnected with the natural world.

Our forebears recognized the energetic significance of certain places in the landscape, which they sometimes marked by the creation of art. Such art has been discovered in the deep dark recesses of caverns in Spain and southern France, dating back up to 34,000 years. These images and the open-air rock art from up to five millennia ago reveal the use of these special places for psycho-spiritual expression.

Environmental research at sites of ancient significance is still in its infancy. But the scientific evidence already amassed strongly suggests that the human–environmental interaction at these places, both natural and monumentalized, may encompass more subtle energetic effects too. Such interactions are known by the few primary peoples remaining on Earth, such as the Aboriginal peoples of Australia, whose geomantic traditions and knowledge of the *Tjurkupa*, or Dreamtime, may go back as far as 40,000 years.

Whilst the modern scientific study of Earth energies is embryonic, the sacred sciences of *feng shui* in China and *vaastu* in India, as well as other forms of geomancy elsewhere, have for millennia studied the subtle energies of Gaia and communed with her Spirit to bring harmony and well-being to people and places. Inevitably, certain aspects of ancient traditions are specific to their cultures and times, but much of what was understood has universal applications and thus is as relevant to us today as it was millennia ago.

Since the 1960s there has been a rising interest in geomancy and a progressive honing of geomantic skills. Today there are national societies of dowsers in the UK, the US and a number of other countries. In Europe the teaching of geomantic traditions to architecture students and others involved in the design of buildings is increasing in popularity – and at an intensely opportune time when our built environment is probably more toxic than ever before and both land and buildings often suffer from geopathic stress.

Geopathic Stress

Whilst our natural environment is both abundant and benevolent, Gaia does produce forms of radiation that can be harmful to us. The meridians of the Earth can also become blocked or imbalanced in some way. Such geomagnetic disturbance is generically referred to as 'geopathic stress'.

Some people are more sensitive to such stress and susceptible to the dis-eases it engenders. This appears especially to be the case when someone is already under stress from other lifestyle factors and their immune system already depleted. Others that are vulnerable and thus at higher risk include young children and old people.

European researchers have led the way in determining the relationships between geopathic stress and human illness. One well-known study was carried out in the 1930s in the town of Vilsiburg, southern Germany, by the dowser Baron Gustav von Pohl. By dowsing the houses of the small town, von Pohl was able, with 100 per cent accuracy, to identify the incidences of cancer amongst its inhabitants. By dowsing the level of geopathic stress in the places where the beds of the cancer sufferers had stood, he was also able to locate where in their bodies the cancers had developed.

One canton in Switzerland now takes the problem of geopathic stress so seriously that it offers a grant towards the cost of a dowser's site survey before the building of any new house. Planning permission will not be granted until this has been carried out.

Geological Faults and Underground Water

Geopathic stress may have a number of specific causes. The two primary subterranean causes of geopathic stress are geological faults and underground water.

The levels of electromagnetic activity generated by the stresses of geological faulting are well known to geologists, who measure the surface level of ionization to identify such faults and thus locate the minerals, including oil, that are often associated with them.

Such ionization, the levels of which increase significantly at night-time, may include substantial amounts of radioactive particles and high-frequency gamma rays – all detrimental to human health. Ongoing exposure to these rays may cause cancer.

Electromagnetic bursts emanating from fault lines may also be a cause of so-called Earthlights, for which there is extensive anecdotal evidence from around the world. The folklore of such phenomena attests to their ability to engender altered states of awareness and visionary experiences.

But the most prevalent cause of geopathic stress is underground water.

Whilst the art of dowsing is indeed best known for the ability of its practitioners to locate such water, there is no as yet well-accepted theory as to how the water gets to be where it is. Geologists now know, however, that etched into the ocean floors of Gaia for many thousands of miles are trenches where rocks are recycled both into and out of the molten magma that underlies the Earth's crust. Seawater, at great pressure, is an integral component of these subduction processes.

Whilst as yet unproven, such pressurized water may find its eventual way through fissures and cracks until it rises inland to near the surface of the Earth. The current theory is that here, due to the localized non-permeability of surface rocks, the pressurized water is unable to escape upwards and is forced to radiate horizontally.

These sites are termed 'blind springs' by dowsers. They generate powerful energies and many have been dowsed as being beneath churches and ancient sacred sites.

However, water is also an amazingly effective carrier of energy. So, if the underground energies are polluted or stagnant, or the water passes through a seam of rock that includes highly radioactive minerals, geopathic stress may result.

Sacred Sites

From the beginning of the Neolithic era, people began to alter the Earth. Natural places that were deemed special were further enhanced and monuments began to be built, often in places of prior significance.

Growing numbers of researchers are now seeking to understand the energetic resonance of these ancient sites. Their aim is to gain a deeper appreciation of their purpose and the sacred science of their construction.

In the 1980s, the Dragon Project, co-ordinated by researcher Paul Devereux, brought together specialists covering a range of scientific disciplines to determine energetic anomalies at sacred sites throughout Britain.

Their preliminary findings identified a range of energetic

anomalies, notably high levels of natural radioactivity, magnetic effects and peaks of ultra-sonic energies at certain times, which suggested the intentional placement of megaliths to mark and possibly enhance these natural effects.

Since then dowsers, Earth mysteries enthusiasts and geomancers have continued to explore such sites, each adding to our store of Earth knowledge.

Spirits of Place

For many researchers, what begins as a scientific search for such knowledge expands into a spiritual quest as the magic of such sites weaves its way into their awareness. And sensitives visiting sacred sites have long reported the presence of discarnate beings there.

Such 'spirits of place' are experienced in many forms. Some appear to be the guardians of the site, having once lived there and been in service to its sacred aims. Others are elemental beings, or Devas, an ancient Sanskrit name meaning 'shining ones'.

We will encounter Devas again in Chapter 12, where we will discuss how to hear their age-old wisdom and learn from them how to diagnose and release imbalanced energies and geopathic stress in the environment. But here we'll share the true story of one group of people who decided to learn devic wisdom for themselves.

The founders of the Findhorn community went one step further than green-fingered gardeners when in the 1960s they began to consciously communicate with nature spirits to co-create a garden on a windswept sandy spit in northern Scotland.

As they had little money, growing their own vegetables was an important part of their lives. But the difficult conditions and impoverished soil made the project daunting and their prospects uncertain.

One of the founders of the community, Dorothy Maclean, began to connect with the plant kingdom Devas and later with the Deva responsible for the local area, a being she called a 'landscape Angel'. Thanks to other clairvoyant connections and their willingness to follow the guidance of their devic mentors, the Findhorn community was able to grow abundant harvests for many years.

Crop Circles

Another harbinger of our changing perception of Gaia and ourselves is the phenomenon of crop circles. To date nearly 12,000 of these 'temporary temples' have been reported around the world.

Their manifestation goes back centuries. But only in the last few decades has the seasonal arrival of vast and intricate formations caused reactions that have ranged from wonder to disdain.

The heartland of this worldwide phenomenon is the landscape of southern England. Here, in the rolling chalkland of the sacred landscape around the great Neolithic circle of Avebury henge and its geomantic partner, the massive mound of Silbury Hill, the most intricate formations have been found.

The creation of crop circles appears to involve electromagnetic vortices and sonic energies. Such energies would need to be coherently focused to create the geometrical and other complex patterns that have been a feature of the formations over the last 15 years or so.

The biological imprints of such energies have also been discovered. The usually microscopic transpiration holes in the stems of affected plants have been found to have increased in size over 100-fold – as though exploded from the inside by the release of high energies. And whilst the affected plants of these living mandalas remain unharmed, the subsequent growth patterns from their seeds show significant differences from those of seeds from unaffected plants in the same field.

The surface soil within crop circles is also affected and geological analysis has shown that clay minerals have crystallized in the same way as they would if exposed to heat and pressure.

Significantly, none of these effects has been seen in control samples of plants and soil taken from outside the formations that have been studied.

But why the circles are created and who the circle makers are remain unanswered questions. Despite the claims of so-called 'hoaxers', the accumulated evidence does not support human agency as their sole and easily dismissible cause. My own perception and that of many other geomancers is that the phenomenon is a co-creation between the realms of Gaia, our collective unconsciousness and possibly extra-terrestrials, and signals the coming Shift of consciousness. If we are prepared to hear its message, this way-shower speaks to us in the archetypal language of symbol and geometric harmony – the language of the cosmic hologram.

In my own experience, by being prepared not only to hear their message but also to listen, I've been repeatedly gifted with intuitive insights and a sense of being nurtured by Gaia. Crop circles have benignly guided me along a path of inner healing, as they have for many others. And with their help I have been further sensitized to subtle energies and the quiet voice of Spirit.

By my willingness to listen, I've found that I have been

able progressively to commune with and receive the wisdom of the devic and elemental beings of Gaia and the aetheric guardians of the ancient sacred sites.

The Unity Grid of Gaia

We are ever-more conscious that the Earth is a living entity. Since ancient times, mystics and geomancers have perceived a 12-fold geometric energy grid encompassing her. I call this the 'Unity grid' because as a holographic microcosm of the universe it holds the ever-present 'memory' of the wholeness of physical creation and resonates with the coming Shift of consciousness and the embodiment of the future destiny of both Gaia and ourselves.

As humanity collectively evolves in consciousness, so does Gaia, and vice versa. And as we expand our awareness, we not only reconnect with Gaia but also resonate with the energies of the Unity grid.

Hitherto, the energy meridians of Gaia have been dowsed as embodying polarities of male and female, positive and negative. Now, however, the 'child' aspect of the fundamental cosmic trinity – its neutral or creative principle – is becoming ever-more active as a new cosmic age is ready to be born.

The Living Earth

Gaia is a living being and, as our planetary home, is our co-evolutionary partner. We have seen how we fundamentally resonate with her cycles and energies and how our holographic inter-relationship is being progressively rediscovered by science. The imminent Shift of consciousness is not only our own collective destiny but that of Gaia and all her realms. As we access the awareness of the

8th and higher chakras, we can re-establish our relationship with her and listen to her wisdom and guidance in these tumultuous times.

Indeed, the more we commune with her, the more we may quieten our own fears and inner turmoil and realize that she and we are fellow cosmic travellers.

In Chapter 12 we'll return to how we may consciously re-establish our relationship with Gaia by hearing the voices of her devic and angelic realms and listening to their wisdom. We'll also explore how to heal the energetic imbalances and geopathic stress to which our environment may be subject.

But now we will explore the matrix of consciousness of our Soular System and discover how the Sun, Moon and planetary bodies also interact with us on profound levels.

CHAPTER 8

Cosmic Waves

The holographic and conscious universe energetically relates to itself at all scales and levels of experience. Each Solar – or Soular – System within it is essentially a group soul, a self-relating hologram within which individual and collective soul experiences are played out.

Our own Soular System, formed four-and-a-half billion years ago, is a wondrous environment for us as spiritual beings to explore physical experience. Research is progressively supporting the probability that physical life was seeded on Earth from space. We also know that the dust of which our system is comprised was created in the death throes of earlier stars – we are truly star seeds.

Our Soular System

Our Soular System is shaped rather like a vast flattish disc with the Sun at its centre and all the planets, including the Earth, spinning around it in the same direction and in roughly the same plane. As seen from the Earth, the orbits of the other planets through the heavens thus remain within a few degrees either side of the path of the Sun, which astronomers call the 'ecliptic'.

Due to the tilt of the Earth on her axis, we actually perceive all the planetary paths and the ecliptic itself as waves that appear to encircle us over the cycles of their orbits.

Ancient stargazers envisaged the outlines of deities and animals in the sky and by about 500 BC had embodied 12 of these in star patterns or constellations along the 360-degree circle of the ecliptic. Each 30-degree section of the sky is known by the name of one of these 12 signs of the so-called zodiac, which form the stellar background to the yearly path around the heavens of the Sun, Moon and planets.

The astrological cycles relating to the zodiac begin with the sign of Aries, against which the Sun rises at the March equinox. They continue with Taurus, Gemini, Cancer, Leo, Virgo, Libra, Scorpio, Sagittarius, Capricorn and Aquarius before completing with the sign of Pisces.

Over time the characteristics attributed to each sign evolved to create what Carl Jung perceived as the greatest tool of psychological analysis known to man. Scientists of the eminence of Isaac Newton and Albert Einstein have also considered that astrological insights offer us profound understanding of human personality.

Here we must emphasize that the Soular System as a holographic matrix of consciousness is self-referential, so the characteristics relating to each zodiac sign represent the influences applying to that section of the matrix and not to those of the much more distant stars making up the zodiac patterns.

Cosmic Re-membering

Astrologically, the Sun, Moon and the five planets that are visible to the naked eye – Mercury, Venus, Mars, Jupiter and Saturn – resonate with our personality-based energy field through the mediation of our seven chakras. Their energetic influences at the time and place of our birth create an astrological chord that is unique to each of us. And over the last couple of hundred years, at the same time as we have progressively come together on a global basis, the outer planets Neptune, Uranus and Pluto have been discovered. These planets take much longer to orbit the Sun than the inner 'personal' planets. So whilst individually we embody their influence, their primary astrological resonances are considered to be on generational and collective levels.

For astrologers, the discovery in 1977 of Chiron, a planetoid whose orbit lies between those of Saturn and Uranus, represented an energetic bridge between the personal and collective psyche of humanity. And this has been interpreted as offering us a key to inner healing.

Such resonance is reflected in the planetoid's name, for in Greek myth Chiron was the wisest of the centaurs, half-horse and half-man, who was the teacher of the great healer Asclepius. Chiron himself had been wounded, but being deemed immortal was destined to carry his injury for eternity.

Also, in October 2002, NASA announced the discovery of the first trans-Plutonian planet, one of a growing number now being found on the furthest fringes of our Soular System and whose origins go back to its primeval fragmentation four-and-a-half billion years ago.

Millennia before the invention of the telescope, Sumerian scholars nonetheless somehow appear to have been aware of *all* the planetary bodies of our Soular System. A tablet of baked clay dating back millennia seems to depict a system comprising the Sun, Moon and a retinue of 10 planets including the Earth – in total a Soular System of 12 bodies. Given that in addition to the Earth only seven astronomical bodies of the Soular System would be visible to the Sumerians, how were they aware of the planets that were in theory discovered only millennia later?

Even more intriguingly, modern astronomy recognizes that the retinue of the Sun comprises only nine planets, including the Earth, not the ten depicted by the Sumerian tablet.

According to antiquarian Zecharia Sitchin and other researchers, ancient Sumerian myths also refer to this tenth planet and a resulting Soular System of 12 bodies. The myths describe the chaos wrought as this 12th body roamed through our Soular System, ultimately causing a catastrophic collision that led to the formation of the asteroid belt. Could the planetoid Chiron be a remnant of this cataclysm and thus an energetic remnant of this 12th planet?

Astrologers view Chiron as bringing forward the awareness of our inner wounding and facilitating our healing on individual and collective levels. Is it that the primeval debris scattered throughout our Soular System as a result of this ancient catastrophe is now emerging into our awareness as the 12th harmonic of our collective awareness, as we become ready to re-member our own dis-membered psyche? For it appears that as we progressively access our 12-chakra energy field of unity awareness, our journey to wholeness is also a journey being undertaken by the holographic consciousness of our entire Soular System.

Our Astrological Journey

As a harmonic matrix of consciousness, all of our Soular System embodies life. The positions of the Sun, Moon and planets within the signs of the zodiac and their relationships to each other at the time and place of our birth form the holographic pattern of influence denoted by our birth, or natal, astrological chart.

Astrologers view this interference pattern of correspon-dences between the archetypal patterns embodied in the

Soular System and individual human consciousness as comprising our personality. And given the specific time and place of our birth, the pattern embodied by each individual is unique.

Astrology is a huge subject and astrologers may spend a lifetime exploring its nuances. Nonetheless, its fundamental principles are straightforward. So let's now discover how these engender the energetic matrix of our personality. For by understanding the energetic influences of each of the 12 zodiac signs, the planetary bodies and the major aspects they make with each other, we are able to gain a deeper understanding of our character and thus empower our ongoing journey of awareness.

Two-fold Symmetry

Within the fundamental 12-fold matrix of the Soular System, the cosmic dance of the Sun, Moon and planets incorporates cyclic waves which embody two-, three- and four-fold symmetries.

There are three primary expressions of the fundamental two-fold symmetry in which various astrological aspects form partnerships and polarities.

The first of these is the partnerships formed between signs that are six months apart and thus face each other across the dome of the sky. Aries is thus partnered by Libra, Taurus partners Scorpio and so on until the sixth partnership, that between Virgo and Pisces. In considering the overt influence of each sign that the Sun, Moon or a particular planet is placed in at the time of our birth, we also therefore need to note the more subtle and yet intrinsic influence of its partner.

The second expression is the polarity of light, as represented by the hemisphere of the sky above the horizon at our birth, and of shadow, the hemisphere below the horizon at that time. Planets above the horizon will have more open influences within our personality, whereas the influences of those below will be subtler.

Thirdly, as there are 12 zodiac signs, beginning with Aries, active and passive attributes can also be attributed to each in turn. So the signs of Aries, Gemini, Leo, Libra, Sagittarius and Aquarius are deemed to embody the active, or male, archetype whereas Taurus, Cancer, Virgo, Scorpio, Capricorn and Pisces carry the passive, or female, principle.

Three-fold Qualities

Three-fold symmetry is embedded by energetic qualities that reflect the innate understanding that all experiences are themselves waves which come into being, consolidate and then fall away. In astrological terms, the zodiac reflects this three-in-one quality of experience in its division into so-called 'cardinal' signs (Aries, Cancer, Libra and Capricorn), which are associated with the initiation of activities, 'fixed' signs (Taurus, Leo, Scorpio and Aquarius), which are associated with their full expression and manifestation, and 'mutable' signs (Gemini, Virgo, Sagittarius and Pisces), which are associated with their integration.

Four-fold Elements

The final division of the zodiac is the four-fold symmetry represented by the embodiment of the energetic characteristics of the four archetypal elements of Fire, Earth, Air and Water. Those of us who have Fire signs in our astrological make-up (Aries, Leo and Sagittarius) are seen as being enthusiastic and outgoing. Earth signs (Taurus, Virgo and Capricorn) are associated with caution and practicality, Air signs (Gemini,

Libra and Aquarius) with clarity of mind and communication, and Water signs (Cancer, Scorpio and Pisces) with sensitivity and empathy.

The Astrological Cycle

The Sun begins each yearly astrological cycle by rising in the zodiac sign of Aries, the ram, at the March equinox. Aries is the active cardinal sign embodying the element of Fire. As such its energetic qualities are those of dynamism, enthusiasm and directness. But for someone with a number of planets in this sign, its energies can be overly expressed as being assertive, aggressive and selfish.

The second sign of Taurus, the bull, is the passive and fixed Earth sign. Its energy is stable, patient and oriented towards security and materiality. Taureans are generally practical and endowed with common sense. However, a chart with planets clustered in Taurus may signal stubbornness and an overly materialistic outlook.

Gemini, the sign of the twins, is designated as the active mutable Air sign, being changeable and communicative with diverse interests. Someone with an emphasis of planets in this sign, however, may be superficial, unable to concentrate on any one activity and easily bored.

The fourth sign of Cancer, the crab, is passive cardinal Water and its energies are emotional, nurturing and intuitive. However, when strongly aspected in someone's chart, it can signify moodiness and the tendency, like a crab, to retreat into its shell when threatened.

Leo, the lion, is the sign of active fixed Fire. Determined and powerful, it needs to express its creativity and to do so openly to be fulfilled. If a Leo is obliged to hide their light under a bushel they are likely to set the barn on fire! And when over-expressed, this sign can be attention-seeking and disruptive.

The sign of Virgo, the virgin, is passive mutable Earth and its energies are practical, analytical and orderly. Whilst able generally to express these energies with intelligence and skill, Virgoans can be hypercritical or prudish if strongly aspected by planets.

The next sign, Libra, the scales, is active cardinal Air. As its archetype suggests, its energetic influences are balanced, diplomatic and concerned with natural justice. However, a surfeit of planets in this sign may result in a personality that is resentful or indecisive.

Scorpio, the sign of the scorpion, is passive fixed Water. Generally with high levels of physical and emotional resources, Scorpionic energies are emotionally intense and if unfulfilled can be jealous or restless.

The sign of Sagittarius the centaur is half-horse, half-man and its energies are active mutable Fire, tending to combine physical strength with a powerful intellect. Expansive and versatile, this sign needs diversity and challenge. A continual seeker, it will become frustrated if its search is curtailed.

The tenth sign, Capricorn the goat, is passive cardinal Earth and is generally ambitious and seeks to do the 'right' thing. Status-conscious and structured, it will set goals and work conscientiously to achieve them, especially in the context of business and career. An over-expression of its energies, however, can result in authoritarianism.

The sign of Aquarius, the water carrier, is active fixed Air and its energies are innovative and individualistic. Often embodied in pioneers, the energies of this sign need both freedom and the company of those of like mind. When strongly aspected, however, its energies may be expressed in unpredictability or eccentricity.

The 12th and final sign of Pisces, the fishes, is passive mutable Water and its energies are compassionate and spiritually insightful. But whilst Pisceans can be inspiring, they can also be overly impressionable and in extremes be addictive personalities.

Sun, Moon and Ascendant

At our birth, the influences of the Sun, Moon and planets each correspond to a specific psychological function or motivation which is then directed by the energies of the zodiac sign in which it is located.

Three of the most significant aspects of our birth chart are the placement of the Sun, Moon and what is termed the Ascendant or Rising sign.

The positioning of the Sun at the time of our birth reflects the outer identity of our personality in this lifetime – like the Sun, it symbolizes how we shine. The sign from which its energies radiate thus indicates how we approach life. The other planets to which it is aspected show us how our sense of identity integrates with the other aspects of our psyche.

The Moon reflects the Sun astrologically, as it does astronomically. It symbolizes our inner feelings and instinctual responses. In our natal chart, its position shows us what we need to feel good about ourselves and thus offers insights as to how we may most effectively respond to life. Its alignments with other planets reveal how our feelings respond to other aspects of ourselves.

The Ascendant isn't a planetary body at all but is the zodiac sign that is rising over the eastern horizon at our time of birth. Its energies influence how we co-create our path through life. It defines the foundation of our personality, how we adapt to our environment and reveals us to ourselves.

Whilst most of us are aware of our Sun sign, as it is the one used by newspaper and magazine horoscopes, understanding our Moon and Ascendant signs is equally significant and crucial for us to gain a balanced understanding of our personality. Appreciating their combined influences enables us to know ourselves better and to balance and harmonize their energies within our psyche and thus our lives.

The Personal Planets

Now let's turn to the planets of our Soular System and their associations with other characteristics of our human experience.

From the earliest times until the 18th century, astronomers were also invariably astrologers. The ancient Greek stargazers gave the planets names that corresponded to their deities and embodied their archetypal presences. The names by which we now know the planets are the later Romanized versions of these Greek gods.

Mercury, the messenger of the gods, is the innermost planet to the Sun and symbolizes communication. Its position in our chart not only represents all the ways in which we express ourselves, but also how we think. It is also associated with travel. When it appears to go backwards, or retrograde, for a period of time, which it does several times each year, communications and travel plans of all sorts are likely to be disrupted. During these periods, it's useful to check details and even, if appropriate, to defer important matters to a more propitious time.

The planet Venus is next out from the Sun and astrologically represents relationships and what pleases us. Generally, in a man's chart, the position of Venus also reflects an ideal female image to which he is innately attracted.

The planetary symbolism of Mars, the Roman god of war, relates to activity, impulses, aggression and sexual drive. In our chart it shows us how we assert ourselves and the nature of our desires. Complementing the position of Venus in a man's chart, the position of Mars in a woman's chart then reflects her ideal male image.

Jupiter was the king of the gods and the planetary symbolism of Jupiter is that of wisdom, expansion and abundance. It contrasts with and partners Saturn, whose influence relates to discipline and limitation. Rather like our out-breaths and in-breaths, their complementary influences enable our lifelong experiences to ebb and flow.

Until the discovery of Uranus in 1781, astrologers based their psychological profiles on the seven visible bodies of the Soular System, which correlate with the seven chakras of our personality energy field.

However, with the discovery of Uranus in 1781, followed by Neptune in 1846 and Pluto in 1930, astrologers were able to gain insights into aspects of our collective psyche.

The Collective Planets

Whilst all the visible planets have orbital periods, from the 88 days of Mercury to the 29 years of Saturn, which lie within the scope of a single human life, the three outer planets, Uranus, Neptune and Pluto, take much longer to orbit the Sun. From Uranus at 84 years to Neptune at 165 years and Pluto at nearly 248 years, their primary influences are thus perceived to be generational and collective.

As the Sun, Moon and five visible planets resonate with us on a personality, or ego-self basis, these outer planets do so on transpersonal levels. In so doing, they thus energetically bridge our sense of personal self and our sense of community.

The discoveries of these outer denizens of our Soular System began at a time when our human family was starting to interact on a global level. Energetically, we may see our collective awareness of Uranus in the late 18th century as triggering the revolutionary overthrow of imperial states, the resurgence of individuality, the early stages of democracy and the entrepreneurial inception of the industrial revolution. Astrologers thus describe Uranus as the great awakener of personal and collective possibilities – but possibilities that may, of course, be expressed in ways that are revolutionary rather than evolutionary.

Neptune's discovery, in the mid-19th century, occurred at a time of re-emergent interest in the psyche. Named after the Romanized god of the sea, its influences arise from the subconscious and can either enable us to gain deeper understanding of reality or escape from it into delusion.

At the beginning of the 1930s, when Pluto's influence entered our awareness, we had collectively arrived at the threshold of an era that may ultimately lead to either our destruction or transcendence. For it was at its inception that we became able to split the atom and therefore capable of global annihilation.

Pluto was the Roman god of the underworld and plutonium was the name given to the then newly discovered element of our potential nemesis. But Pluto also indicates our power to destroy old behaviour patterns and regenerate new ones. Its astrological influence is transformational. Currently Pluto is aligned with the centre of our galaxy and it is this, as we shall discuss a little later, which astrologers consider is one of the harbingers that offer us transcendent opportunities for a Shift in consciousness.

The Wounded Healer

Between the orbits of Saturn and Uranus lies the orbit of the planetoid Chiron, the wounded healer, who is supporting us both personally and collectively on our journey of re-membering ourselves.

The position of Chiron in our birth chart identifies which areas of our lives and psyche are dis-membered and offers us the opportunity to reconcile the polarities and behavioural imbalances we carry. However, if we continue to project our personal suffering onto others, or indeed the world generally, Chiron's influence is unable to be effectively expressed. Acknowledging our wounds and consequential suffering and taking responsibility for our own healing are the first steps in allowing Chiron to guide our path to wholeness.

The orbital period of Chiron is just below 51 years. At certain times during our life, it is harmonically aligned with its natal position in our chart – as are all the planetary influences. When these 'transits' occur, they very often correspond with major life experiences and turning points.

In our late 40s and early 50s, when Chiron's influence equates to – conjuncts – that of our birth, it offers us an opportunity for profound healing and inner growth. Indeed, we may even find that unless we take advantage of this cosmic offer, our lives will become unsustainable until we do!

Just as Pluto is now aligned with the galactic centre, at the time of the discovery of Chiron in the late 1970s, its Ascendant was similarly aligned. The influences of both these astrological bodies are thus crucial to this current era of transformation.

Aspects and Transits

We have seen how consciousness expresses itself as energy and that all energies are waves. In an astrological chart, harmonic alignments between planets, where their waves of influence combine in certain ways, are called 'aspects'.

Throughout our lives, as the intricate cycles of our Soular System continue to resonate with our individual consciousness, there are times when the planetary aspects of our birth are recreated. These periods, which may last from less than a day to many months, are, as we have seen, called transits. Whilst their influences are similar to those of our birth chart, our responses to them reflect the level of our current awareness.

Issues that were previously unresolved and hopes we may have abandoned return at the next round of these spiral dances for us to review once more. We may then continue to play out old patterns or we may utilize the opportunity to make inner and outer changes in our lives.

There are six primary aspects that astrologers consider to be especially significant: conjunctions, oppositions, trines, squares, quintiles and sextiles.

Planets are said to be conjunct when they are in the same position or very close to each other in a chart and their energies combine. Depending on the nature of the planets involved, such conjunctions can be supportive or challenging, but they will always be powerful, as the influences of the planets concerned are conjoined.

Opposing planets, in contrast, occupy positions that are diametrically opposite to each other in a chart. They embody an innate tension until our awareness allows us to come to terms with and balance their inherent polarities. We may play out an opposition aspect in our chart by identifying with one planet and either denying the qualities of the other in ourselves or projecting them onto other people. It is only when we are willing to embrace both qualities that we are able to balance their energies.

The influences of planets in trine aspect, where they are 120 degrees apart, are harmonious and their flowing energies denote abundant support for the areas of our lives they impact.

Square aspects, in contrast, are when planets are 90 degrees apart and they produce conflict that usually requires effort on our behalf to resolve. However, such challenging alignments may be the motivation we need to undertake inner growth.

Quintile aspects are formed by planetary bodies being 72 degrees, or one-fifth of the circle of the sky, apart and reveal the areas of our lives in which we are powerfully driven. Such inner drives are often subliminal and can be discerned through compulsive tendencies and personality traits. Quintile influences empower us to succeed and under-standing them enables us to do so in ways that are healthy and balanced.

Finally, sextiles, where the planets are 60 degrees apart, have a harmonious and easy-going influence. Such aspects in our chart suggest we will avoid conflict and seek compromise in our lives. The specific planets involved in such an aspect will determine in which areas of our lives such compromise will be sought.

Precession

The Earth continually wobbles on her axis and this creates the phenomenon known as the 'cycle of precession'. Travelling backwards through the zodiac, over a period lasting nearly 26,000 years, the Sun rises at the March equinox against each of the 12 signs in turn. These 12 Ages, each lasting 2,160 years or so, are named after the zodiac sign whose sector of the sky influences the energetic characteristics of that Age. We are now transitioning from the Age of Pisces to the Age of Aquarius.

Astrologers debate how the influences of each era manifest in our collective psyche. One view, to which I myself adhere, is that the wave of zodiacal influence giving its name to an Age begins during that era but only finds its full expression in the one following and falls away during the third. Thus the coming Age of Aquarius will seed the influences associated with that sign, Piscean characteristics will find their full expression and those of the Age of Aries will fall away.

These energetic influences then embody further nuances due to the harmonic relationships between them and the zodiac signs characterized by the same quality and archetypal elements. So in the Age of Aquarius we should individually and collectively begin to experience its characteristics of personal empowerment and co-creation, the full expression of the Piscean influence – seeded by the great teachers of 2,000 years ago – of compassion and spiritual wisdom, and the falling away of the self-focus of Arian energies.

2012/2013

As we undertake the transition to the Age of Aquarius, however, metaphysical prophesies and portentous astrological align-ments are currently culminating in a way which suggests that the period of 2012/2013 may herald a major Shift in our collective consciousness.

The 12 signs of the zodiac represent the psychological attributes of their sector of the sky. However, unknown to most people is that there is a 13th constellation which lies on the ecliptic, called Ophiuchus.

The ancient Greeks knew Ophiuchus as Asclepius. He was the god of healing, the son of the Sun god Apollo, and learned his healing arts from Chiron. This 13th zodiac sign is depicted as a man holding two serpents, representing the balanced and re-membered energies of our psyche. In some traditions this 13th archetypal figure also represents the perfected human being or soular hero.

But not only does this archetypal figure lie on the path of the Sun, its location in the sky also aligns with the centre of our galaxy.

As we have seen, both Pluto and Chiron are also conjunct with the galactic centre at this momentous time.

At this exact moment too, for the first time in nearly 26,000 years, the cycle of precession has brought the Sun at its December solstice – the traditional birth of the soular hero – into alignment with the 13th zodiac sign of Ophiucus, Pluto, Chiron and the galactic centre.

What does the resonance of these amazing astrological and archetypal portents reveal as we journey towards the time of its culmination?

According to the ancient Mayan priests, who were masters of time, to fulfil our collective destiny we would undergo a Shift of consciousness at the December solstice of 2012 – and so their calendar ended on this date. They were unable to intuitively perceive what would come afterwards and how the very nature of our experience of time would continue.

My own view and that of exponentially increasing numbers of people around the world is that we are being offered an incredible opportunity for a collective expansion of awareness that includes not only ourselves but also Gaia and our entire Soular System.

The higher chakras of our unity energy field are now becoming accessible to us. The 8th chakra of the universal heart is our portal to transpersonal perception. The 9th or earthstar chakra is linking us with rediscovered reverence to Gaia and all her children. And as we begin to access the 10th chakra, we are also reconnecting at a conscious level with the archetypal awareness embodied by the Sun, Moon and planets of our Soular System.

This re-connection is also a re-membering. As we've seen, astronomers are currently discovering the fragmentary members of our Soular System. The nature of the cosmic hologram is such that as we are re-membering ourselves, the Sun, Moon and the nine planets of our Soular system are now being reconciled with the fragments of their – and our – 12th family member.

Beyond the Soular System, the 11th chakra is connecting our awareness with galactic consciousness. The story of its initial activation on 23 December 2003 and our ongoing journey towards 2012/2013 will be told in my forthcoming book *The 13th Step*. Such awareness is, I believe, our collective destiny.

As we've seen, the astrological support for this Shift of consciousness is abundantly available to us. But only we can undertake this leap by choosing to commit to our own healing and thus to the healing of the whole.

In the third and final part of *The 8th Chakra* we'll explore how we may undertake this journey and reach our ultimate destination: HoME.

PART III

Be

CHAPTER 9

Heart-Centered Soul Healing

Our human experience has sometimes been described as spiritual boot camp, a view with which, I suspect, most of us would concur. Our journey in the physical world involves us in challenges that often bruise and hurt us, not only bodily but also mentally and emotionally.

For many of us, the traumas of these non-physical bruises may take a lifetime – or more – to heal. At their most extreme, our psyche is fundamentally dis-membered. And it may then be a long and arduous inner journey to re-member and heal ourselves.

Such traumas show up as imbalances in our personality energy field, but we may only be consciously aware of a small fraction of them. Like icebergs, the larger part may lie hidden in the depths, buried in the habitual responses of our subconscious.

Depending on what aspects of our life and experience such a trauma primarily affects, and the characteristics of our personal response, it may engender blockages in one or more chakras and manifest as specific types of physical ailments. But as the personality of our ego-self is energetically mediated through all seven chakras, imbalances will ultimately affect us on all energetic levels.

Archetypal Traumas

In Chapter 6 we discussed how archetypal and collective consciousness is an integral aspect of our individual soul experience. Across all cultures and throughout history, archetypal myths and symbols have reflected our common heritage. Archetypal patterns of behaviour are a collective experience with which we all identify. The same is true of archetypal traumas.

There are five fundamental traumas – abandonment, abuse, betrayal, denial and rejection – which we all embody to some degree or other. For the great majority of us, it will be one of these primary patterns that we recognize in our own life as repeating cycles of experience and pain. And whilst it may have been triggered by events in this lifetime, we may well have played out the same archetypal theme in other lives.

All five archetypal traumas are engendered on physical, emotional and mental levels of experience. Abuse, for instance, does not have to be physically administered – it can be imposed on emotional and/or mental levels too. And we can be abandoned on emotional levels as catastrophically as if we had been physically deserted.

In our experience of these patterns, we are inevitably both givers and receivers. For instance, if we embody the archetype of abandonment, we will not only be abandoned but in other circumstances will be the one who is abandoning someone or something. Ultimately, we will abandon ourselves.

All archetypal traumas work in this way, though each primary archetype has its own associated patterns of behaviour through which we both play out its archetypal essence and also seek to avoid or cope with its consequential trauma.

Triggering in Childhood

For most of us, in our current life, such an archetype is likely to have been first triggered when we were very young children. In my experience of healing work with many hundreds of clients, the ages when such initial triggering occurs range from when a child is developing in the womb through to about five years old.

At such young ages, we are developing our sense of self and are vulnerable to the traumas of what in hindsight may be trivial events. But at the time, our ability to articulate and make sense of what is happening is limited – often we cannot yet speak – and so we respond by internalizing the pain at a subconscious and cellular level.

For instance, until about 30 years ago in the UK, when a child needed to be hospitalized, its parents were limited to only short visiting hours. For many children this engendered a deep sense of loss and abandonment. Even though in their adult years many such children have been able to rationalize their experience, their emotional trauma was embedded at subconscious levels and they are still struggling to come to terms with its legacy. Accordingly, they experience continuing occurrences of the abandonment pattern in their lives, often without understanding why.

Can we then even begin to comprehend the sense of loss and abandonment of children such as entire generations of Aboriginal children in Australia, taken from their families without warning or exception and fostered in cultures both alien and often hostile? Or the children orphaned through conflicts around the world or by the ravages of Aids?

Puberty

As young children we are inherently open to the emotions of

those around us, especially those of our parents and siblings. So to take another example of an archetypal trauma, if our parents are playing out a pattern of abuse, even though we may not be its direct subject, we can nonetheless take on and embody the essence of its pain. Throughout childhood we may then experience situations that engender the same archetype.

Also, as I have found from working with many clients, during our early teens, as we struggle to make the transition from child to adult, one or more significant events almost always occurs which deepens the imprint of the archetypal pattern. And by our late teens, our responses and coping mechanisms have generally become habitual.

It is therefore unsurprising that there is an innate correlation between the severity of an archetypal trauma in an individual's life experience and issues relating to their sense of self-worth.

Before we go on to consider some of the behaviour through which we either play out these five archetypal patterns or try to cope with their consequences, there is one important fact to emphasize: as we enact each pattern, not only do we perpetrate it on others, or them on us, but we ultimately impose it on ourselves. Whilst we may do this overtly or subconsciously, it is this which may be the most persistent means by which our lack of self-esteem is reinforced.

Abandonment

Abandonment is all about loss. An alternative way we describe it is to say that someone has been deserted. Indeed, if we close our eyes and envisage the emptiness of a geographical desert, its loneliness and desolation offer us a sense of how it feels to experience this archetypal pattern.

The diverse means by which we seek to cope with abandonment all try to avoid such loss and the consequential pain and loneliness. For instance, when we are either in a new relationship or at a point in an ongoing relationship where we have a choice to take it to the next level of intimacy, we may find ourselves sabotaging it in some way. Thus, and probably at a subconscious level, we aim to leave someone before they leave – or abandon – us.

Alternatively, we may seek to control or manipulate others to avoid loss. This may occur not only in how we relate to other people but also to our surroundings and to life in general. Indeed, if we feel particularly vulnerable to the possibility of abandonment in our relationships, we may become even more concerned about exerting control over other aspects of our life. Depending on our personality, we may choose to control these areas of our life on an openly directive level or we may instead be less direct and more covert in our attempts to manipulate circumstances.

Almost paradoxically, we may alternatively attempt to avoid even the possibility of abandonment by isolating ourselves instead. In this way, we ensure our own imprisonment by shutting out life itself and thereby abandoning even ourselves.

However, the reality of life is that it is a process of continual waves of change. When we are able to embrace rather than fear its inevitability, it is able to flow freely through us and we are able to move on. But when we seek to control the flow of change, we dam the river of life – with often unforeseen and sometimes tragic consequences for others and ourselves.

As with all five archetypal patterns, the first step in coming to terms with abandonment and resolving and releasing its energetic trauma is our acknowledgement of its presence. Whilst our awareness of its influence and our responses to it may be at subconscious levels, we can know its reality by its continuing occurrences in the relationships and circumstances of our lives.

The Illusion of Separation

As spiritual beings undertaking the challenges of a physical experience, the abandonment pattern that many of us carry has been triggered by the feelings of entering physical incarnation and the illusion of separation from Spirit.

Often, souls who suffer this have chosen a purpose in this life that engenders not only a great challenge but also a great opportunity. For this illusory schism is the cause of the deepest sense of abandonment we can feel. By healing its trauma within themselves, these souls offer a great gift to our collective psyche.

Many incarnate into families where there is an extreme manifestation of this archetype. Their courage in recognizing it and struggling to heal it for themselves and those around them is all the greater in that they have ultimately chosen to undertake this work. And as their inner process involves not only their re-membering of that choice but also bridging their perceived schism with Spirit, the essence of their healing is a homecoming of profound joy.

The abandonment archetype can be particularly painful as we consider either our own death or that of loved ones. Ultimately, each and every one of us has an eventual appointment with the death of our body and thus the opportunity to move on to our next cosmic adventure. However, for those of us who embody the archetype of abandonment and for whom the physical world is all we perceive, death may represent the ultimate abandonment and we may thus fear it at a deep level that we may not consciously even understand.

Being helped to see beyond the limitations of the physical world and to realize that Spirit never abandons us can often be the breakthrough to the beginning of our healing journey.

Grief

When we do, however, suffer the loss of those closest to us, our need to grieve is natural and necessary. By allowing ourselves the time and circumstances to acknowledge and eventually release the sadness of grief, we are able to move forward. But when we deny ourselves the opportunity, our sadness doesn't go away, but is merely subdued.

When we lose someone, by being able to talk about them and shed tears of memory, we can acknowledge both that we miss them and celebrate the experiences we shared. Whilst we consciously remember the past, however, we are often unaware that our feelings of grief are also for the future that we will not be able to explore together. So when we grieve, it's important for us to acknowledge these past, present *and* future aspects of our sorrow and, by our tears and our gratitude for having experienced the presence of the loved one in our lives, to enable the grief to flow though us as it needs to for us to be able to reconcile our loss and to walk on.

Abuse

The cruelty of deliberately inflicting pain can operate in ways both overt and subtle. From the physical humiliation of corporal or sexual abuse to the emotional and mental abuse caused by constant unconstructive criticism, this pattern is one that can literally leave the deepest scars. It can be a means of making ourselves feel better, however briefly, by making others feel worse. More than any other, this archetypal pattern continues to play out within families on an inter-generational basis.

Those of us who have been subject to abuse, especially as young children, may feel somehow that it is our fault, for we are generally taught to believe that the adults close to us are 'right', and so, by default, we are 'wrong'.

Abuse is also a pattern of behaviour in which the person inflicting it will tend to justify their actions, both to themselves and others. Alternatively they may be in denial that they are actually abusive.

When we abuse ourselves, often as an extension of the abuse of us by others, we most often do so through the insidious pain of addiction. Many people initially turn to something to which they later become addicted in an attempt to escape other forms of abuse. Sadly, escaping the abuse of others is usually easier than escaping such self-abuse once its influence has been imprinted on our psyche.

Betrayal

The treachery of betrayal, whether of one's friends, family or nation, is one that strikes at the very heart of how we relate to each other. Being able to trust those with whom we share our lives answers deep needs for inner security which, as we have seen, lie at the very root of our being.

Betrayal destroys trust and demolishes loyalty. And of the five archetypal traumas, all of which were suffered by Jesus, the one from which we all recoil is his betrayal by Judas Iscariot.

Yet Judas had an inner motivation for betraying his spiritual leader. Whilst the Bible suggests his reasons rather than offering details, the archetypal pattern of betrayal has as its inevitable corollary the fact that the betrayer feels justified, on whatever basis, for the act of betrayal. Those reasons are diverse and may not even be known on a conscious level to the betrayer themselves. They will, however, be intimately associated with how they perceive themselves in relationship to the person or institution they betray.

To betray or be betrayed by someone, we need already to have been involved in some form of relationship with them – we can't be betrayed by a stranger. This is the case even when a nation is betrayed, for it is everyone of that nationality whose trust is betrayed. But some degree of disillusionment with the existing relationship almost always precipitates the act.

To begin to understand betrayal, we need to be able to *listen* to the self-justification of the betrayer – whether that is someone we feel has betrayed us or our own justification in betraying someone else. Whatever the rationale, however specious, it offers clues we can use to gain understanding.

Whether we are the betrayed or betrayer, it offers us an opportunity, if we are able to muster the courage and honesty, to search our own behaviour and motivations. For, as we have seen, the cosmic principles of consciousness reveal the correspondences and reflections that mirror our inner and outer circumstances throughout all our experiences.

Denial

Denial is the unwillingness to acknowledge the reality of a situation, either about others or ourselves. Whilst it is an archetypal pattern in itself, it may also be a component in the process of coming to terms with and healing the other patterns we are discussing.

Often, to prevent any chink forming in the armour of denial, anything that may initiate such acknowledgement will be avoided at all cost. Thus the old adage 'Out of sight out of mind' is a primary behaviour pattern of denial. Certain subjects are taboo, we will studiously keep out of the way of certain objects or situations and we may develop obsessive or habitual behaviour that prevents the possibility of bringing to mind what is being denied.

Prejudice is invariably associated with denial. For by seeing someone or something in the way we think they are rather than the way they actually are denies their reality. Such prejudice usually enables us to feel superior and thus better. But it also denies our own reality.

A pattern of denial by its very nature renders it difficult to address. As addiction councillors always relate, until someone has hit rock bottom, in some cases to the extent of losing their families, livelihoods and almost their lives, the denial that they have an addiction continues to play a large role in its continuation.

But once such denial is released, healing can begin.

Rejection

The final archetypal trauma we will consider is that of rejection – the refusal to accept or acknowledge something or the discarding of it as worthless.

If we are embodying such an archetype, we may consider that nothing is ever good enough. Ultimately, that often includes ourselves, and thus we are unable to accept and love ourselves for who we are.

Alternatively, when we encounter rejection, rather than perceiving it as the judgement and projection of others, we may take it to heart and thus feel inherently worthless.

As with all the archetypal traumas, rejection influences us on the levels of our lower three chakras and thus affects our fundamental sense of self. Continual rejection leads to progressive isolation, or ice-soul-ation. As we separate the 'I' of ourselves from the 'not I' of all others, we turn to I-ce! We are then frozen and literally unable to flow. We may feel as though our soul is encased in ice and we have no warmth – no love – in our lives. For ultimately, it is only love that enables us to thaw and be released into the flow of life once more.

Family Patterns

Whilst we experience such archetypal traumas in our individual lives, being innately collective we very often find that the same pattern runs through our close family – grandparents, parents and siblings.

As our consciousness is holographic, when we become aware of and committed to the inner healing of our own energetic patterns, we essentially gift that healing to those with whom we have shared its inter-play. This may have profound implications, because often such family patterns go unacknowledged and unspoken. We enter into dynamic and dysfunctional relationships where there develops ways of being and behaving to which everyone involved has adjusted their own psyche in their own way.

Compensation in other circumstances can be beneficial, such as when the loss of, say, sight or hearing is counter-balanced by increased sensitivity in other senses. But compensatory behaviour to cope with archetypal trauma merely enables the trauma to deepen its energetic imprint on our individual and collective psyche.

Healing Schisms

As these archetypal traumas are intrinsic to the holographic nature of polarity-based consciousness, we can also discern them in the psyche of entire groups of people who share an ethnic, religious or cultural heritage.

For instance, for over two millennia, the diverse peoples of the Balkans have undertaken tit-for-tat aggression. Whilst the ferocity of their conflicts has ebbed and flowed over the centuries, the underlying mistrust and resentments between ethnic and religious groups have been energetically imprinted at a deep level of the collective psyche.

In other areas of the world, such communal traumas also remain unresolved, with each new generation being culturally impregnated with the same prejudicial fears and hatred as their forebears.

The Middle East is a primary example of this. Here the schism between Arabs, Jews and Christians symbolically and energetically dates back nearly four millennia. At the time of the biblical patriarch Abraham, his two sons, Ishmael and Isaac, by two different wives, Hagar and Sarah, are deemed to have formed the bloodlines of the Arabic and Jewish people respectively. The later schism between Jews and Christians also ultimately arose from a Jewish unwillingness to accept the bloodline and thus authority of Jesus as the Christ, which was, however, embraced by his followers and the resultant Christian faith.

Now in these transformative times, as we are becoming able to access the energies of the 8th and higher chakras, our expanding awareness is able to discern and understand these ancient patterns within ourselves, our families, communities and nations. And even more significantly, by aligning with the consciousness of our transpersonal awareness we are now able to facilitate the healing of their associated traumas.

Intention

The word 'heal' has the same origin as the word 'whole'. So essentially, when we heal, we become whole. And as harmony is the natural state of the world, so disharmony should alert us to imbalances and a lack of authenticity and integrity in our lives.

The inner journey to harmony and wholeness is one we can all tread. But the first step is the acknowledgement that there is an imbalance. The second step is the intention to do something to change. Without that intention, our perception has no energy to draw on to enable the flow of that change to begin.

But the choice inherent in such intention may initially not arise at the conscious level of our ego-self. Indeed, its impetus is far more likely to originate at higher levels of our integrated consciousness. We may first become aware that such an intention has been set by the fact that our personal circumstances become even more difficult! Whatever archetypal pattern we are embodying, we may find that somehow it gets a whole lot worse. And if we were not aware of the pattern before, we surely become so now.

This is the means by which our higher-self draws our attention to such a pattern and indicates that its continuation in our lives has become unsustainable. If we don't get the message, our circumstances will usually continue to deteriorate until we do!

When we finally do 'get it', however, we can energize our intention to change on a conscious level and then take the next step. As we then continue the process of healing, according to the nature of the holographic Cosmos and its cosmic principles of manifestation, our outer circumstances will change to correspond to our inner states. By changing from within, we transform our lives from the inside out.

Neale Donald Walsh made this clear in his book *Conversations with God*. He turned our usual mantra of (fill in the details of your own grumble): 'When we *have* ... we will *do* ... and we will *be*...' into the opposite order of 'Be ... do ... have.' In other words, we must 'be' what we choose to be first and not last!

Understanding these principles and applying them to our own life circumstances offers us a profound insight into ourselves from which we can move forward.

A Good Question

You might be asking by now, why does our higher-self choose the embodiment of such archetypal patterns and their consequential pain? A very good question!

The answer is, for the same reason that any good actor relishes a challenging role. The actor knows that at the end of their performance, they take off the costume and make-up and go home. So, too, our soul knows that at the completion of our physical experience we are re-united and thus aware of our soul's purpose. And, like an actor having triumphed in their role, we can afterwards enjoy the kudos for our remarkable performance.

Our experiences and how we deal with them make up the performance of our lives and define who we are. But if we over-identify with our role, we may hold on to feelings and ways of thinking that are simply part of the play. To fully participate in life, we need to feel, and we need to have thoughts of all hues. However, when we are unable to allow these to flow easily through us and instead carry them with us, they become ever-heavier energetic baggage and prevent us from moving forward. Then we begin to recycle the patterns they embody ... and recycle ... and recycle...

The five archetypal patterns we have discussed are incredibly rich in the diversity of opportunity they offer to explore polarity-based consciousness and thus the illusion of separation. Accordingly, the resolution and healing of such patterns also offers us both individually and collectively a fast track to wholeness. Yet paradoxically, we often hold onto the pain of the traumas we incur – many times until the tipping point where the pain of holding on is even greater than the fear of letting go.

In such a case our pain can be our comfort blanket, although we would probably deny this. Whilst honouring anyone who takes their pain to the wire before letting go, I would nonetheless encourage all of us not to wait for such despair before we take a leap of faith into the unknown.

Seed-Points

In order to release the traumas of such patterns from our psyche, understanding the events that 'seeded' them and thus energetically releasing their imprint from that point can offer healing at a profound level.

Whilst the experiential seed-points for archetypal patterns tend to be triggered during childhood, especially in the pre-school years and again at puberty, as we grow to adulthood we become enmeshed in the patterns and our progressively habitual responses become the rutted road of our lives.

But such a triggering may in actuality be a retriggering. In my healing experiences with very many clients, we have together realized that such patterns, especially when deeply rooted, have their originating seed-point not in this lifetime but in another life.

We have already referred to the richness of these patterns in exploring polarity consciousness. Although the themes of each are the same, there are vast opportunities for diversity in their expression. And so, as we begin to understand our own pattern in this life, we may come to recognize that we have played out the same archetype in many other incarnations.

However, as we shall see, by accessing our higher awareness, through the portal of the 8th chakra we are able to identify the energetic seed-point of the pattern and its retriggering in this life – and to release and thus heal its imprint in our psyche.

Integrated Medicine

Traumas, as we've seen, are held at different energetic levels and thus to effect their release we need to undertake a holistic approach to healing. Usually only a small part is held at cognitive levels. Most is held subconsciously, resulting in responses that may not yet have been acknowledged or understood on a conscious level. However, when even a small aspect of the archetype rises into our waking awareness, it is a sign that healing is ready to commence.

Integrated medicine is now being rapidly acknowledged as the most effective means of bringing together different modalities to support a person's specific needs. This emerging approach to health combines an aim to prevent dis-ease through education and awareness of the implications of lifestyle choices with a holistic approach to treatment. Utilizing the most up-to-date technologies for detecting dis-ease or treating physical injuries, it embraces complementary therapies for chronic illness, the alleviation of pain and the energetic release of blockages. It is also progressively recognizing our holographic nature and the relationships between thought, emotions and physical ill-health. And increasingly, elements of integrated medicine are modalities to release trauma from our energetic biofield.

Energy Medicine

All techniques of energy medicine utilize the same underlying principles of resonance and ultimately the eight cosmic principles we discussed in Chapter 4. However, it's not the energy that heals, but the information and perception it carries. Thoughts and emotions are information-based patterns of energy configuration and it is the rearrangement of these patterns that either inhibits or restores health.

The many techniques of energy medicine which unblock and release trauma therefore aim to provide free-flowing meridians which will then enable the reprogramming of our harmonic patterns of belief and behaviour.

Many new techniques are currently emerging and over the past few decades there has also been a reappraisal in the West of the ancient Eastern techniques of energy medicine such as acupuncture. Whilst in general such techniques require qualified practitioners, the principles of energy medicine empower each of us as individuals, for there are simple and effective techniques that we can all use.

The benefits of regular meditation practice that realigns us with cosmic harmony are well known. And we have seen how the ancients also recognized the healing power of sound and music. The fundamental harmonics expressed through the toning of many Eastern mantras – the simplest of which is the *Aum*, the expression of primordial cosmic creation – is an everyday means of aligning our energies with the flow of all life.

A number of new techniques are being developed which are intended to release the energetic patterns associated with past emotional or psychological trauma. On an energetic level, these therapies usually work *within* the personality energy field – essentially at the same level of ego-based awareness at which the trauma was initially incurred. If, however, the issues that gave rise to the symptoms are embodied in archetypal energetic patterns, the symptoms will return unless the underlying attitudinal and behavioural patterns have been amended and the mental and emotional reasons for the imbalances fully resolved.

In other contexts, it has often been said that it is impossible to resolve a problem from the same level of awareness that created it. This is also true when attempting to resolve and release mental issues and emotional blockages. Essentially, if we continue to think, feel and act in the same way, we will continue to experience the same outcome.

However, by energetically raising our awareness to the transpersonal level of the 8th chakra of the universal heart, we are not only able to witness and understand the pattern from a higher perspective but also, by connecting with our higher-self, to gain guidance on the most effective means of releasing it.

When we climb a hill, we are able to see further than when we remain in the valley below. So when we perceive ourselves from the vantage point of the 8th chakra, we can witness, with intuitive insight and compassion, the journeys of our lives and the traumas that it is now time to release.

The 8th Chakra

Accessing the energies of the 8th chakra enables us to become aware of the deeper behavioural patterns that pervade our lives.

Where these no longer support us, we are then able to attune to the wisdom of our higher-self and undertake universal heart-centred healing at a soul level.

As we have seen, the triadic energies of the 8th chakra bring together the awareness embodied by our personal mind, heart and will and raise their vibrations to a transpersonal level.

Within our ego-based self, the fundamental role of our mind is to maintain the perception that each of us is a separate individual and to sustain the illusion of the polarities of the physical world. The continuing role of our heart, however, is to ensure that we do not wholly forget that in fact we are all connected and ultimately One. And the purpose of our will is to optimize the role we play in co-creating our realities by our willingness to participate in the play of life.

The more we participate, however, the more we tend to identify with the role we play. Such identification is not by itself a problem. It's only when we become or remain attached to the implications and consequences of such identification that our experiences imprison us.

This is where the level of awareness of our personal mind, heart and will embodies our identification and their associated traumas. In coping with them, our conscious mind may seek to protect us by taking control. We may then attempt to retreat from future pain by closing down the inner voice of our heart or by refusing to listen to the creativity of our will. The pain we're accustomed to can then be rationalized as preferable to the pain we fear we may incur if we 'let go' and leap into the unknown. Unfortunately, what our ego-mind perceives as protection may in fact be imprisonment.

When, however, we access the awareness of the 8th chakra, we are able to see the archetypal pattern in which we have been enmeshed. We can perceive, without fear or judgement, its themes, including its triggering in this lifetime and its possible seeding in another life.

Balancing and manifesting the healthy expression of the seven personal chakras takes us from the loneliness of separation and loss to the embodied sense of self – our perception of our alone-ness. However, as we go on to explore the higher transpersonal chakras of the universal heart and beyond, we will move on from being al-one to re-membering that we are all-one. An ancient name for God was *El*. So as we re-member who we really are, we go from being al-one to all-one by adding an 'l' – or 'el'. In other words, we consciously embody the God within us.

Scientists have discovered that the nature of the cosmic hologram enables the expression of the maximum amount of awareness to be embodied within spacetime. The incredible diversity of life and the uniqueness of individual awareness then ensure that this capacity is fully utilized for the physical embodiment of experiences. For ultimately the purpose of our integral consciousness – our soul – in choosing to be here is to co-create and to learn.

As we heal our ego-based persona, we are able not only to expand our awareness but also to embody such co-creativity and increasing understanding as a member of the comm-unity of all life.

The Intention to Heal

We can only to make the choices for our own healing in the present moment. When we revisit the past as part of our heart-centred soul healing, we do so only to bring an understanding of how our patterns and blockages were created in order to discuss how best to release them.

Only by resolving and clearing the energetic imprint at its seed-points, both in this life and, if it was the case, in another life, can we ultimately release its influence. For unless we address the root cause of the pattern, wherever and whenever that may have been seeded, its effects will continue to spread into our lives.

As with any energy-based healing, and indeed any energy work generally, we also need to ground our awareness in order to fully embody and integrate our healing experience. As we've seen, it is through our root chakra that the grounding of our personality-based awareness is accomplished. However, as we access the higher vibrational energies of our unity chakra field and begin to work at a soular level, we need to ground our awareness through the ninth, earthstar chakra.

When any behavioural or other pattern is released, on an energetic level it leaves a void behind. A fundamental attribute of all energy, however, is that any void will be filled. So unless replaced by another form of energy, the void left by the release will then fill up with whatever other form of energies may be present. By always replacing the energy that has been released by the energy of unconditional love, we both balance the intrinsic flows of consciousness within ourselves and offer ourselves the greatest gift of unity awareness.

As you read and integrate the message of *The 8th Chakra*, you are already undertaking universal heart-centred soul healing. And on page 251 you'll find a simple meditation which will help you to access and embody these higher vibrational energies.

Let's now go through a number of ways in which we may

recognize and release these outworn traumas.

The Traumatic Seed-Point in This Life

The first step is for us to recognize the energetic seed-point of the pattern in this life.

To do this, always begin by silently breathing in to the 8th chakra and intending that your highest guidance reveal clearly to you the circumstances of the occurrence of the seed-point.

Your higher-self may then offer you an inner vision or a feeling or sense of something, or a memory may pop suddenly into your awareness.

Your higher guidance can present itself in many ways – it may appear 'real' or surreal, couched in symbols or flashes of colour – but the significance lies in what it specifically means to *you*. Whatever comes forward and in whatever form, trust that it is purposeful and allow yourself to listen to its message.

If nothing appears, relax and allow the process to unfold.

The Energetic Seed-Point

An alternative way of revealing the seed-point is to breathe into the 8th chakra and inwardly intend that your higher-self guides you back along the timeline of this lifetime. Allow your intuition to guide you until you stop at a particular scene or become aware of a specific memory.

Breathe into the 8th chakra and allow the events of the memory to unfold. Remember that *your* way of perceiving may mean that you sense or feel this inner exploration rather than visualize it. But however your higher guidance offers its gift of deeper understanding, it is right for you.

As your understanding emerges, continue to breathe through the 8th chakra and inwardly ask that your higher-self guide you to a full understanding of the seed-point experience.

When you are intuitively aware that you have this understanding, ask your higher-self what you need to do to heal its energetic imprint in your psyche.

Inner-View

Whilst when you are fully in the energies of the 8th chakra, you are able to witness this unfolding of understanding with compassion and without judgement, you may well find that painful or heavy feelings do initially arise. If they do, breathe into the 8th chakra and allow the feelings to flow through you.

You may visualize this by seeing or sensing the energies being held in a particular part of your body. If you do so, again allow your breath to flow though the 8th chakra and sense the blockage dissolving and the heavy energies flowing down through the earthstar chakra beneath your feet and into the Earth. As you sense them doing so, offer gratitude to Gaia for their release.

Don't leave an energetic void in their place, but visualize or sense the energies of unconditional love flowing through the 8th chakra to that part of your body.

The Release of Heaviness

In identifying the seed-point of a pattern in this lifetime, you are very likely to encounter family members, friends and others with whom you have played out this pattern. Those who are fundamental to your experience will emerge into your awareness. You are also able in your inner vision and sensing to call those people to you. As you do so, breathe into the 8th chakra and allow your highest guidance to flow through you, revealing to you what you now need to do to heal the pattern.

It may be that you need to have an inner dialogue with whoever has appeared to you.

Remember that you are able to call upon their higher-self in the same way that your own higher-self is intrinsically guiding you throughout this process.

Speak directly to them, and say what you need to, with loving truth and without holding back. In return, listen to what they have to say to you, for you may gain a profound understanding of their motivation and in so doing a deeper understanding of their own pattern and compassion for their pain.

Loving Truth

This inner dialogue alone may enable the pattern to be released from your psyche. But if more is needed, ask your higher guidance to reveal how to proceed.

When you sense that the pattern has been released, feel into your intuitive awareness to confirm that it has been freed at its seed-point in this life. With a very deep pattern, you may find that as you remain open, other circumstances may arise. If they do, go through the same processes to release each one. However, by intending that you release the pattern at its seed-point, it will be to that point that your perception will be drawn.

During this process you may, however, find that whatever you do or say, those whom you call to you or encounter are unwilling or unable to meet you in this crucible of consciousness. If that is the case, acknowledge it, honour their choice and allow them to go.

You are both still energetically connected by the archetypal pattern, however, and so to heal you need to free yourself and the other person from its constraints. If they are unwilling or unable to communicate with you then you may ask your higher guidance how to best accomplish this.

One way that often works well is to envisage where in your and their body or energy field you sense that you are joined by an energetic thread. This may be head to head, or left knee to right elbow! Or it may be via particular chakras.

Whatever appears, trust the guidance it offers. Then, as you breathe unconditional love through the 8th chakra, envisage that the thread is released – again, by whatever means you are intuitively guided to do so.

When you sense that you are released, feel into your intuitive awareness to confirm that this is indeed true. As previously mentioned, with a very deep pattern, you may find that as you remain receptive, other memories arise. If they do, go through the same process of releasing their trauma.

However, as you continue to intend that the pattern is released at its seed-point, your awareness will intuitively come to that originating event to be healed.

Honour and Allow

Seed-Points in Other Lives

When an archetypal pattern is released in this lifetime, in order to prevent the possibility of its reappearance, the energetic template of its original seed-point needs to be healed and released in the life in which it was initiated.

The holographic nature of the Cosmos means that healing at the level of this original seed-point enables the release to flow through every life where the archetypal pattern has been enacted and into the Now.

In understanding the seed-point events of another life and healing their legacy, you don't alter history. You do, however, increase your level of awareness and thus transform your

If you are ready to perceive the other-life seed-point of the archetypal pattern you have been embodying, begin by accessing the energies of the 8th chakra. Intend that your higher guidance is revealed to you and open yourself to whatever comes.

Whilst you may find that your awareness arises in ways that are similar to those you experienced whilst understanding and healing the archetypal pattern in this lifetime, don't assume that this will be so. It may be that your perception of the originating seed-point comes to you in a very different way. So just relax and be open.

You may find that the circumstances of the seed-point life are revealed to you in detail. Or, more likely, you may perceive a specific scene or event. Remember that you are in conscious control of this cosmic DVD, so breathe through the 8th chakra and allow your higher-self to guide you to the level of understanding you need to enable the healing and release you intend.

present and your future.

Freeing Ourselves

Being in the energetic vibration of our 8th chakra also facilitates the identification of other imbalances and traumas within our psyche and guides us in understanding how to free ourselves from limiting beliefs and fears.

To do this, you may find the meditation on page 251

The clarity and focus of your intention is fundamental. So before you begin, you may wish to consider what you are asking for.

When you have accessed the energy of the 8th chakra, as you breathe through it, focus your intention and inwardly speak it, allowing its purpose to resonate within you.

As with healing the energies of archetypal patterns, your identification of limiting beliefs and how to heal them may arise in many different ways. In the healing energies of the 8th chakra, whatever is revealed is the gift of your higher-self. Trust it.

helpful.

Heart-Centered Soul Healing

From the higher vantage point of the 8th chakra of the universal heart, we are able to heal the archetypal traumas of abandonment, abuse, betrayal, denial and rejection not only for ourselves but for our entire human family. Their re-soul-ution is an intrinsic aspect of our inner healing. Such healing – our journey to the wholeness of who we *really* are – is a step-by-step process. As we have already seen, ancient myths refer to this as the quest of the solar – or soular – hero.

These wisdom teachings perceive that the wholeness of the human soul embodies an integrated 12-into-13 harmonic of fundamental energies. We are thus microcosmic reflections of the cosmic harmony that is comprised of the musical scale of 13 notes.

On a larger scale of the cosmic hologram, this harmony resonates through the yearly dance of the Sun, Moon and Earth, comprising 12 solar months and 13 lunar months of Full Moons. The paths of the Sun, Moon and all the planets of our Solar – or Soular – System through the sky also interweave through the 12 signs of the zodiac each year, creating the matrix of astrological influence of our individual and collective awareness.

Ancient wisdom relied on metaphor and myth to depict this understanding. So in the journey of the soular hero we repeatedly encounter these archetypal numbers.

The journey of the Sun, or Sol, is thus the journey of the soular hero. And the journey of the soular hero is the journey of the soul.

Now is the time for us to real-ize that we all have the potential to be solar – or soular – heroes. Whilst each of us follows a unique path, we all share the ultimate destination of the soular hero – the real-ization and embodiment of the unity that transcends and gives birth to all polarity-based consciousness.

The journey of every soular hero incorporates 12 steps that sooner or later, we all tread. It is this journey that we'll now explore together.

CHAPTER 10

The Journey of the Soular Hero

Life is consciousness exploring itself. How can it do this other than through the processes we call experiences? How can experiences unfold other than through change?

Change is the only constant in life. Yet we often treat it as a foe, seeking to barricade ourselves against its inevitability. Change is not an enemy at the gate of the citadel of our identity, however – it's the friend that accompanies us on our journey home. By embracing it as a friend, a fellow traveller and guide throughout our journey, we are able to flow with the river of life rather than to dam and thus stagnate its waters.

Change is a friend who challenges and surprises us, yet nonetheless only wishes our highest good. Mother Teresa once expressed her feelings in a way that I suspect finds an echo for most of us when she said that whilst she understood that God never gave her anything greater than she could handle, she only wished sometimes that He didn't trust her quite so much!

The changes in our lives always offer us opportunities to co-create and to learn, however. They form the stepping-stones of our path of inner growth and are the way-showers of our journey to wholeness. For nothing happens by chance and everything has a higher purpose.

Twelve Steps

Whilst the ultimate destination of this journey of self-realization is the same for all of us, the steps we take to reach it are unique to every one of us. The path we choose to take may be one of the well-worn ways of the world's great religions or it may be a path less trod. We may also choose to stop at any point along the inner journey as it becomes more arduous or challenging.

But regardless of whether our choice is a spiritual highway or a little-trod by-way, if we do decide to walk on, something incredible happens: we begin to notice that whilst our journey is unique, there are universal way-stations along the path, way-stations that nurture us and validate our onward direction.

Such way-stations are embedded in every initiatory tradition and healing process. In many traditions the insights they embody are deemed to comprise 12 steps, which together form the 13th and thus become complete. And as we embody the spiritual understanding that each step gives to us, we too become whole.

These insights were revealed to me during my own soular journey, a three-year pilgrimage to 12 locations around the Earth which will be related in my forthcoming book *Many Voices, One Heart*. Here I'll share the lessons I and my fellow travellers learned. I've introduced some of these insights already in this book, but here we may see how together they comprise the steps that lead to our individual and collective re-membering.

My own soular journey continues, for having been offered the map of the terrain, I feel that I'm still reconnoitering and rediscovering it every day of my life. With each thought, word and action, I have opportunities to embody its cosmic truths and take sanctuary in its spiritual way-stations.

In experiencing extraordinary revelations, I feel ever more ordinary. And in the ordinary moments of my daily life, I perceive the divinity that *is* the world.

I fall over too, with occasional days when I take refuge under the duvet, and yet I experience other days when miracles, like butterflies, alight on my shoulders from dawn until night. Unlike the time before I began consciously to undertake the journey of the soular hero, every moment now is precious and every day offers me anew the infinite magic of life. And I now know for myself the insights that the mystics of all ages have shared with us.

But this adventure is not mine al-one; it is ours all-one. The newly available energies of the 8th and higher chakras are our communal heritage, and their embodiment our communal destiny.

Let's now share what I and nearly 70 fellow travellers discovered as we undertook the journey of the soular hero.

The First Step: Responsibility

Our first step is to take responsibility for our choices and their resultant implications and consequences.

A fundamental choice taken by our soul has been to incarnate here on Earth at this time. Each and every one of us has taken this decision.

This is a bold statement that people react to it in different ways. Some are able to acknowledge such a choice. For many of us, however, the challenges we experience in our own lives and those that we see in the lives of others lead to our denying the possibility.

Yet, as we have seen, our consciousness is integrated on all levels of awareness and we make choices not only at the level of our ego-mind but also at the level of our higher-self, as in the choice to incarnate. Until our awareness expands, however, we may only perceive the choices that emanate through our ego-mind.

Our awareness is continually changing. It is different today from yesterday. And it was different last week from last year. We are only able to make choices in the present moment and with our present level of awareness. Nonetheless, we may find ourselves saying 'If only I knew then what I know now.' Whilst we may often berate ourselves for lacking that awareness, it's like grumbling that a three-year-old child doesn't know how to send an e-mail. Actually, that's probably a poor metaphor, as I suspect a few three-year-olds can do just that!

Taking responsibility lies in making choices with the awareness that we have in the present moment. We don't need to take responsibility for the choices of our higher-self, unless we are aware of those choices. We need only to acknowledge that we are indeed responsible for the choices we are *consciously* aware of.

We can choose to take this first step of the journey of the soular hero at any moment of our lives. We don't have to wait until we're older, cleverer or richer, have more time or feel happier.

Like all other choices, this too has implications and consequences. For by taking responsibility for our conscious choices, we inevitably expand our awareness. We begin to perceive, in ways both obvious and subtle, the choices we have made and continue to make – choices of which we've hitherto been unaware.

This is the moment to re-mind ourselves, if we need to, not to regret the choices of our past. We made those at the level of our past perception. And the experiences relating to those choices brought us to our current level of awareness.

Having taken this first step, we are also able to perceive that continuing to make the same choices that we've made in the past will lead almost inevitably to the same outcomes. So if we want to change the future, we must change the present.

The Second Step: Fear – or Love?

The second step of the journey of the soular hero is to choose love rather than fear, in thought, word and deed.

When we're in a state of fear, research has shown that our body contracts – we literally withdraw into ourselves, ready to fight or flee. We've evolved such mechanisms as a means of survival. However, many of us are burdened by fears on an ongoing basis, even when there is no immediate or realistic danger. Such chronic fear may be expressed as a specific phobia or embodied in more general ways, such as a fear of commitment or of attaining success. At best, it limits our ability to participate fully in life and at worst it debilitates and locks us in a prison of our own making.

This is *our* fear. We own it, for ultimately no one else can make us fearful. Whilst of course there are people who deliberately seek to instil fear in others, they can only succeed if those others allow themselves to respond in that way. During the Second World War the British leader Winston Churchill once distilled this truth when he said, 'All we have to fear is fear itself.'

How do we relate to the people around us – with love or through fear? For most of us, our partners, friends and families are our 'loved ones'. During the horrendous events of 9/11, the last messages from the people who died on that day were of love, to their parents, wives, husbands and children. But beyond these 'loved ones', how do we relate to the wider human community? Is it with love?

By 'love', I mean an attitude that perceives the world as an inter-related whole, an attitude that looks for the things that we have in common rather than those that apparently separate us. Such love is not blind to the circumstances of the manifest world but is able to perceive, however elusively, the holographic harmony and purpose that underlie and guide them.

Whereas the energies of fear are innately those of scarcity and separation, the energies of love are inherently those of abundance and relationship. But this kind of love isn't always easy to feel for those we perceive as different from ourselves, and fear is often our more immediate emotion. In the dynamics of human relationships, and given the often violent and abusive heritage of our ethnic, cultural and religious diversity, we have much to do to reconcile and heal.

This reconciliation can only begin within each of us. But, as we'll see in the next chapter, it is on our willingness or otherwise to do so that our collective destiny is founded. We live in momentous times that portend great change. As Martin Luther King once said, 'We either swim together as brothers or drown separately as fools.' We cannot resolve the global issues that confront us by acting independently. Unless we are able to begin the process of *authentic* co-operation and collaboration, no single family, group or nation will have a sustainable future.

Individually and collectively, we can respond to the known risks and unknown possibilities either fearfully or with love.

The love we're discussing is not 'soft'. It doesn't collude or compromise with fear-based actions. But it does have compassion and seeks understanding for those that perpetrate them and it does aim to empower those in fear to discover a more loving way of being.

Such a discovery can only come about if those who are more aware are more loving themselves. We cannot say, 'Do what I say, not what I do.' As individuals, groups and nations, unless we ourselves are lovingly authentic, we cannot hope that others who are less aware can become so. The energies of our intentions and motivations, as we've seen, direct the outcomes of our choices and actions. Energetically, the end never justifies the means. For the means *becomes* the end, and we are deluding ourselves if we think otherwise.

Love Isn't 'Like'

But how do we choose love rather than fear?

First, loving someone or something isn't necessarily the same as liking them. We like someone because they resonate with us on a personal basis. Essentially, we *like* someone because they are *like* us.

I mean by this that we tend to like people who share our personal values or view of the world, rather than similarities in our personal likes and dislikes. When we like someone on this basis, it's easier for us to move from liking them to loving them.

Sometimes, however, on a personal level we may find ourselves loving someone despite not actually liking them. In my experience this most often happens within families when we feel that we have very little in common with a brother, sister, parent or child, and yet we love them.

Indeed, as we've seen with the archetypal traumas we play out in our lives, it's very often in family relationships that the greatest traumas are embodied. Such pain is deepened by the fact that it is associated with those we feel should be our nearest and dearest.

In Chapter 5 we explored how as we awaken our perception we progressively access and balance our personal chakras. If we remain at the level of awareness of our lower three chakras, we will continually be seeking security, pleasure and power – and the feelings we have towards other people will be based on that perspective. Only when we awaken and balance our heart and higher chakras are we able to begin to feel love. Otherwise what we might call 'love' is in fact based on control of some sort. Love doesn't seek to control – it seeks to support.

Such love, whilst not necessarily needing us to like the recipient of its focus, nonetheless remains personal. When we begin to access the energies of the 8th chakra of the universal heart, however, the love we feel for others transcends personal love and becomes com-passion. We start to experience the profound interconnection of the entire Cosmos, and in doing so, we see ever-more clearly that fear arises from the illusion of separation. We also see opportunities to heal that fear by feeling the love, both in our own lives and in the wider world around us.

And as we continue our journey to inner wholeness, step by step we attain the reality of love that is unconditional.

The Third Step: In-to-Great

The love embraced by the aspiring soular hero isn't blind. It sees the diversity of the dance of light and shadow that pervades the world and everything in it. But it does so with compassion.

Most of us, although not all, would prefer to see ourselves in the best possible light. Our behaviour may incorporate archetypal patterns that we may deny or rationalize, but I suspect there are few people who when they look into the mirror each morning see someone they consider to be 'bad'. Nonetheless, we all incorporate the relativity – or the real-ativity – of light and shadow. The third step of our soular hero journey is to acknowledge such polarities within ourselves. In so doing, we can begin to embrace their reality, resolve their imbalances and become whole.

When we embody an energetic imbalance within ourselves, often at a level below our conscious awareness, we may feel as though something is missing in our lives. This feeling of loneliness is our way of expressing the loss or non-attainment of inner wholeness. We may seek its fulfilment outside ourselves, especially through relationships. Where we enter into relationships on this basis, we may well discover that the loneliness felt by our partner has played a role in their need for the relationship too. Yet, whatever our motivations, our relationships nonetheless offer us ongoing opportunities to heal.

However, someone or something outside ourselves can never compensate for our inner sense of loneliness. Only when we recognize this and look inwards do we have the opportunity to take the steps from being lonely to being fully ourselves – or alone.

Whereas when we're lonely we feel something's missing in our lives, when we feel alone we empower ourselves. Exploring such aloneness, our true sense of self, is a fundamental aspect of our human experience.

Continuing to aspire to inner healing and greater awareness, though, we reconnect with and re-member ever greater aspects of our soul. And as we integrate ourselves – or, as my dear friend Kelly Daigle says, 'in-to-great' ourselves – we journey from loneliness to aloneness and then on to all-one-ness.

The Fourth Step: Show Up!

The fourth step of our soular hero journey is to embody coherence and alignment with the flow of the Cosmos and our own higher purpose. Our higher-selves offer us the opportunities to explore such experiences every day. But we must 'show up' by being willing to do so.

By opening ourselves to our own higher guidance, we base our intentions on the understanding of our highest purpose – that of our soul. We are thus empowered to embody our destiny in this life, whatever it may entail, with awareness and joy.

If our highest purpose is that the circumstances of our lives remain as they were before, we are nonetheless inwardly transformed and our attitude to them is transcended.

But whether our outer circumstances remain the same or change out of all recognition, our highest purpose in being here is revealed to us and we become able to share our unique gifts in service to all.

The Fifth Step: Now

The cosmic hologram is co-created in each moment. And it is only in the cosmic gift of the present – the Now – that we make our choices and experience our lives. Yet it has been estimated that at least a third of our energies, as expressed through our thoughts and emotions, are focused on the past and a further third are focused on the future. This leaves at most only a third of our energetic attention on the present.

Holding on to the energetic patterns of the past results in regret, grief or anger. In extremis, we may replay its events again and again without resolution or release.

Alternatively, by projecting ourselves into the future we may either seek an illusory escape from the challenges of the present or focus our fears onto unknown circumstances.

Whatever the past has held for us, it is history. We can't change it, although we may judiciously, as we've seen, gain greater understanding of it in order to illuminate the present and heal the future. And we can only influence that future by the choices we make in the moment of the Now.

The more enticing our future might look, the more we might be tempted to ignore the present. Conversely, the less positive it might appear, the more we might retreat in fear – often into the safety of the past. But to participate in our lives, we must live them as authentically as we can. If we were able to predict or guarantee the future, it would be like reading the end of a book or play. If we were able to know the outcome of our lives, why would we pay attention to the intervening events?

As we walk through our lives, by physically only being able to place one leg in front of the other, we retain our balance. Similarly, by being able to perceive no more than the next 'step' of awareness ahead, we keep our spiritual balance. This enables us to make our choices with our greatest awareness.

And so this fifth step of the journey of the soular hero – to live in the Now – is one that we take every moment.

Wave Being

Many of us view life as a race – we even call ourselves the 'human race'! We run from experience to experience, deadline – not lifeline – to deadline, and convince ourselves that this is how we must live. Even when we are chronically exhausted or stressed to breaking point, we may still continue to push on rather than taking a step back and confronting our choices.

Western materialism has persuaded vast numbers of us that such frenetic lives are the only way to be, and that 'more of' and 'newer model' are signs of health and abundance.

If this were the case, however, our level of happiness and health would surely be greatly higher than that of our parents and grandparents. Yet every study over the last few years has shown that in general, our physical, emotional and mental well-being is collectively less than theirs.

Nonetheless, as we have noted throughout *The 8th Chakra*, at this moment of crisis, our higher awareness and that of the Cosmos are enabling us to re-member ourselves, if we choose to do so. We can then transform our race into grace.

Our own higher-selves are offering us the understanding of how to transform 'our way of being' into our becoming a 'wave being'. If we choose to do so, we can enable ourselves not merely to 'go with the flow' but to *become* the flow.

The Sixth Step: Mutual Respect, Love and Gratitude

The sixth step on our journey may be a great leap for many of us. Over the last centuries, religious authorities have informed us that we may only approach the Divine through intermediaries. Science has gone further and insisted that the Divine itself is illusory and that only we and perhaps a few higher animals are conscious. The insights and experiences of the ancients and primary peoples have been decried as superstitious nonsense. And anyone able to connect with the archetypal consciousness of Devas and Angels has been treated with derision at best.

But, as we've seen, science and Spirit are beginning to be reconciled. And ever more people are experiencing directly the realities that mainstream media and out-dated science continue to ignore or decry.

So this is now our choice: do we continue to be part of the materialistic problem or can we become part of the integrated solution?

Choosing to embody our integral awareness is, however, a choice that comes with increasing responsibility. For we know that as we expand our awareness and access the energies of our higher transpersonal chakras, we reconnect to the multi-dimensional consciousness of Gaia, our Soular System and the Cosmos. We do these higher beings – and ourselves – a disservice if we do not acknowledge that we are all fellow travellers. Mutual respect, love and gratitude are key to these spiritual relationships. In continuing to learn and grow, such beings are our loving mentors and spiritual guides. They are not our masters, nor do they ask or wish to be. All they ask is that we embody our destiny.

The Seventh Step: Hear and *Listen*

As we develop a dialogue with our spiritual mentors and our own higher-selves, we will progressively be able to hear their and our own intuitive guidance. How to not only hear but also actively *listen* to this wisdom is the next step of our inner journey to wholeness.

In my own experience over many years, I've discovered that the wisdom emanating from these higher realms invites rather than instructs, is inclusive rather than exclusive and speaks to our sense of service rather than our sense of self. Such wisdom seeks to empower us. It encourages us to embody our own highest purpose and offers us the opportunities to do so.

In the past there have been very good reasons why all initiatory journeys, especially that of the soular hero, have been travelled step by step. For if our ego-self remains imbalanced as we access higher energies, we open ourselves not to the highest guidance but to low levels of consciousness that play on our sense of ego-based importance. This has been why well-intentioned and wise gurus and teachers have accompanied their students along the paths of spiritual initiation.

Now, however, as we become individually and collectively able to access the newly available chakras of our unity energy field, our higher-selves have ensured that we are only able to do so when we are ready. This readiness is expressed through the letting go of our ego-based attachments.

Unlike seekers of the past, who were able to achieve a certain level of 'me-powerment' by force of egoic intellect or will, we are only empowered to access the universal heart of the 8th chakra when our higher-selves know that we are ready. Our conscious willingness to undertake the healing we have explored in *The 8th Chakra* brings us to that point of readiness.

The Eighth Step: Loving Truth

When we sing in tune, we describe the notes as being 'true'. In the same way, when we embody our truth, we are essentially being 'in tune' with ourselves. The cosmic principles through which consciousness explores the holographic Cosmos then ensure that we are true to not only ourselves but to all.

The eighth step of our journey is thus to be authentic and lovingly true with ourselves, all our relationships and the wider Cosmos.

To be lovingly truthful is to be both loving and true, and we need to embody both to take this next step. Sometimes we may perceive the truth of something but be unwilling to express it because we don't want to hurt someone. Whilst we may perceive our choice as being loving, it actually disconnects us at some level with that person. For instance, we may see a friend acting in a way we find uncomfortable. Yet to maintain our friendship we choose not to say anything. Instead we may seek to ignore or deny their actions or we may distance ourselves from them.

Two very dear friends of mine realized that they were taking this approach with each other. Eventually each recognized that every time they felt they couldn't say something, their relationship had taken a step backwards. As their relationship became progressively distant, both were dismayed. Finally, one day they had a heart-to-heart talk and all that had been unsaid was expressed. In that moment they made a commitment to each other that they would say whatever they felt they needed to in order to remain true to themselves – and to each other.

The way they were able to talk heart to heart was, however, crucial. Each chose to speak in the loving energy of truth rather than to blurt out their disagreements. And each was able to listen to the other's truth, even where they felt that it was misunderstood or misguided.

Loving truth is not acquiescence; it is not passive. Neither is it blind, dumb or deaf. It does involve listening to others' points of view – which they may not be able to express in loving ways.

We can make the choice to be lovingly true with both those we hold dearest and with strangers. Emanating from the heart, especially from the universal heart of the 8th chakra, such loving truth can never hurt someone. It expresses our truth of feelings and situations that they may not consciously wish to hear, but it offers them the gift, if they choose to accept it, of a deeper understanding of themselves. Their choice then is to whether to be lovingly true themselves.

The Ninth Step: Discernment

There is an old saying, 'Don't judge another person until you've walked in their shoes.' Yet how many times do we find ourselves judging others without understanding their reasons for acting the way they do? And can we ever believe that we know someone well enough to make such judgements?

There is an important difference, however, between judgement and discernment. When we discern that something doesn't feel right or appropriate to us, we're recognizing or seeing a situation on the basis of our own truth. Whilst our truth may not agree with someone else's perspective, we can nonetheless choose to be authentic in expressing our truth in a loving way.

However, when we judge someone or something, we project our own views onto that person or situation. To remind us of the implications of this truth, Jesus said, 'Judge not, lest ye be judged' ('Do not judge another lest you yourself be judged').

Whereas judgement raises barriers that often result in greater misunderstanding and exclusion, discernment enables us to set appropriate boundaries. Understanding the difference between the two and embodying discernment rather than judgement is the ninth step on the journey of the soular hero.

The Tenth Step: Honouring Experience

Each and every step we take in our quest to be soular heroes is crucial to the completion of our journey. As we become able to transcend judgement whilst recognizing discernment, we are enabled to take the tenth step, which is to honour all experience without condemning, condoning or colluding.

This step may sometimes feel like the *Mission Impossible*

TV programme and films. You may recall that at the beginning of each mission, the intrepid heroes are told, 'Your mission, should you choose to accept it...'

We too may choose to accept or not, and some of our spiritual missions may seem pretty impossible. But personally I don't believe any of them are. A comment by Mother Teresa is one I hold in my heart – that we are never given, or indeed give ourselves, a greater mission than we in fact can accomplish.

Certainly, whatever it brings, the journey of the soular hero is never boring! Every day our higher-selves and the Cosmos offer us interesting, intriguing and irritating ways of understanding and taking this step towards greater awareness.

Honouring our experiences is being able to acknowledge their purpose, even – and perhaps especially – when it is elusive. Honouring is a way of respecting the intentions of our higher-selves and recognizing the integrity of our consciousness. Honouring both our personal and collective experiences in this way is not only fundamental to releasing our traumas, but also helps us to forgive both others and ourselves, and thus to reconcile the past and become able to move forward with a lighter heart.

The Eleventh Step: The Golden Rule

The 11th and penultimate step of our journey is one that, again, Jesus sought to show us. It has been described as the 'golden rule', for it is the most precious of wisdoms. When we are able to live by this simple yet profound precept, we truly embody our wholeness as we real-ize that we are all one.

The golden rule asks us to treat others as we would ask to be treated.

Throughout our history, the most traumatic events have

occurred when we have ignorantly or wilfully discounted this highest of guidance. Inevitably, the cosmic principles have then played out the tit-for-tat implications of our choices.

In the eternal Now, the universe is co-created anew. In this moment, as you read these words, you can choose for yourself.

The Twelfth Step: Cosmic Service

We are now at the threshold of the 12th step, the taking of which brings us to our destination as soular heroes. As we look at ourselves, we notice something. We don't *look* any different from when we started. But as we take this final step, we *see* ourselves for the first time. We see that we are whole and that we are all-one. In the self-awareness of our soul, we understand at last, and with unconditional love, the incredible fragility and yet awesome strength of our ego-selves. And we know now how to transmute the small me-powerment of a fearful ego into the great empowerment of self-realized cosmic service.

The 12th step is our embodiment of the cosmic service of our soul.

The Journey of the Soular Hero

The 12 steps taken by the aspiring soular hero are more of a dance than a journey, in that they are rarely sequential. They involve retracing our steps as we begin to embody the deeper understanding they bring into our awareness.

As in a dance, the lighter we are on our feet, the better. Such lightness is expressed by taking the cosmic dance seriously without taking ourselves seriously. The more we can laugh at – and with – ourselves, the more we can open our mind, heart and will to the rigours and challenges that lie along the way.

But before we continue to spiral upwards as we re-member our soul, let's reiterate our perception of these 12 steps of the cosmic dance of wholeness:

- Accept responsibility for our choices.
- Choose love rather than fear.
- In-to-great light and shadow and see beyond their polarities.
- Consciously align ourselves with the flow of the Cosmos.
- Live in the Now.
- Respect the conscious Cosmos and all its realms.
- Intuitively *listen* to our higher-selves.
- Express loving truth.
- Discern rather than judge.
- Honour all experience without condemning, condoning or colluding.
- Enact the golden rule in thought, speech and action.
- Embody the em-powerment of cosmic service.

We live in an unprecedented time of transformation, so let's now look at how we may be of empowered service as we face our collective challenge to overcome the patterns of history and give birth to a new cosmic age.

CHAPTER 11

Comm-unity

Over the last few years, the Human Genome Project has sought to map the sequence of our DNA. Amongst a plethora of unexpected results, it has revealed that there is a greater range of genetic disparity amongst an average family group of chimpanzees than amongst the over six billion members of the entire human race.

Our physical features, and the racial and ethnic attributes that are the lynchpin of so many of our prejudicial fears, all arise from minor differences between us that together only account for a minute proportion of our entire genetic make-up.

Tracing back archetypal genetic markers throughout the global population has also led researchers to conclude that the earliest modern humans arose 150,000 to 200,000 years ago from a tiny group probably numbering only a few thousand. Since then, our continual interbreeding has related every one of us to every other one – we are all blood kin.

The human family is built on our fundamental unity as a race. Its richness of expression arises not from our genetic heritage but primarily from the interactions of our personalities and the circumstances of our environments and cultural diversity.

The three primary waves of consciousness that form the harmonic essence of our ego-selves comprise the biological template embodied in our genes, our personality and our environment. It is their interactions, both within us and with others, that are the basis of our individuality and of the diversity of our collective human experience.

Influences

Albert Einstein, Isaac Newton and Carl Jung were all advocates of the interaction of the Soular System with human psychology – the ancient science of astrology. And as we explored in Chapter 8, astrology offers profound insights into our personalities and generational and collective influences.

An ongoing 20-year study of children in the UK also considers that the greatest difference between how individual children behave and interact with the outside world appears to arise from the variations in their personalities. The researchers have investigated children with the same environmental influences by studying siblings, both twins and those of different ages. They have concluded that from birth, a child's personality is the most significant factor in determining how different individuals relate to similar circumstances.

The third wave of influence that moulds our human experience is comprised of environmental factors, which on personal and collective levels are incredibly diverse. The family and wider cultural and ethnic heritage into which we are born influence us in ways both profound and trivial and on conscious and subconscious levels. As we mature and explore life, our changing circumstances then form powerful wave-guides for our inner and outer growth.

Or they may not, because, as we've seen, we may choose to retreat into habitual responses rather than deal with the new challenges that we encounter.

Memes

In the holographic Cosmos, our personal human journey is a microcosm of that of the entirety of the human family. Each of us is unique, for consciousness is ever creative. Yet ultimately we share a common heritage and a collective destiny. We all experience the challenges and the joys of being human. We all struggle with our fears and cry out with love. We all hope and we all despair.

Our ego-selves, however, offer us their individual perspectives on the wider world by labelling people, objects and situations. Such labels incorporate factual and experiential awareness but also assumptions, beliefs and perceptions. The more complex are replete with psychosocial and organizational associations. Such labels are termed 'memes'.

In the same way that our genes make up the spirals of our DNA and thus form the blue-prints of our physical body, the memes we embody make up the template or world-view through which we emotionally and mentally perceive the Cosmos.

Memes assemble our present reality from the memories of the past. So we regularly attempt to familiarize the unfamiliar by attaching to such new situations and people the memes of our embedded awareness. The labels we use are thus rich with associations. So when we encounter something or someone new to us, we may 'sum them up' before even knowing what they are really like.

Every one of us is born into a certain cultural heritage whose memetic world-view we inherit. As we grow as individuals, our awareness expands and we may then to some degree or other either embrace or reject the memetic norms of the culture into which we are born.

Our own level of awareness, expressed through our individual personalities, ultimately forms the basis for whatever world-view we ascribe to.

SpiralDynamics

As a human family, we are growing up individually and collectively. But, as in any family, the awareness of different members is at varying levels. The development of perception on both personal and communal levels is not a linear process but occurs in waves whose interactions are complex and diverse. In *The 8th Chakra* so far, we've explored some of the dynamic processes by which we as individuals expand our awareness.

In an attempt to understand how disparate organizations and cultures as a whole grow and develop, in the 1980s American psychologist Clare Graves pioneered an approach termed SpiralDynamics. Since then it has been substantially developed by Don Beck, Christopher Cowan and others. The basic premise is to model cultural and generic world-views as a spiral of developing levels of awareness.

The model subdivides the world-views encompassing the totality of contemporary human society into eight levels. Each embodies a psychology particular to that level of awareness, eliciting certain beliefs and feelings, social, economic and political groupings and cultural norms of values, motivations and goals. Each, Beck and Cowan argue, emerged historically in response to life conditions that became progressively more complex. However, importantly, the levels are neither rigid nor static. Essentially, each forms a wave of increasing awareness, and each incorporates the intrinsic characteristics of a wave in its commencing, peaking and falling away phases.

The generic attributes of the eight levels of what is called the SpiralDynamics integrated – or SDi – model are summarized below, based on the book by Beck and Cowan of the same name.

Beck and Cowan chose colours to label each level in order to render such labels as neutral as possible and thereby minimize value judgements and facilitate the appreciation of all eight levels as authentic expressions of human experience. Indeed, the healthy expression of each of the eight levels is perceived as contributing to the health of the whole spiral of human awareness and development.

The Spiral of Awareness

The SDi model considers that all of the eight levels are responses to increasing complexity and can be discerned throughout historical processes.

The *Beige* level is archaic and, like the focus of our own lower chakras, is dominated by the basic motivation to survive. Whilst this level now involves only a small minority of the human population, it re-emerges in times of extreme stress such as during war or famine.

The *Purple* level is characterized by tribal communities of extended kinship. It expresses its world-view through magic and ritual and is thereby sustained by a profound awareness of the interweaving of life and its mystery.

The empires of old embodied the *Red* level of awareness, being authoritarian, hierarchical and exploitative of others. This level honours heroes and myths and requires communal evidence of respect.

The **Blue** level is generally conformist and loyal to what is perceived as group truths. Dissidence or heresies are feared and seen as betrayal.

Individualistic and oriented to material success and personal advantage, the **Orange** level rebalances communal conformity with regard for personal needs and rights, but often with less emphasis on the associated responsibilities.

The **Green** level seeks to balance the needs of the individual with those of the community and operates from a humanistic viewpoint. The importance of people in general, their feelings and social care are stressed and communal concerns are emphasized.

These first six levels are deemed to form a first tier of awareness and are primarily descriptive of historical world-views. The seventh and eighth levels then form the first two expressions of a second tier of awareness that is now unfolding. These are the Yellow and Turquoise levels.

The **Yellow** level of awareness is the first of a series of levels able to adopt multiple perspectives. It is oriented towards integration and takes progressively integral views of the Cosmos. Generally open to change, it is characterized by systems thinking, where the whole is seen as being greater than the sum of its parts.

The emergent **Turquoise** level is now being embodied in the world. Focused on global wholism, spiritual interconnectivity and the purposeful nature of life, it reconciles heart and mind and is aware of the holographic nature of the Cosmos. This eighth level is emerging as the energies of the 8th chakra now become available to us. Unsurprisingly perhaps, its colour, turquoise, is the one which many people who are accessing the 8th chakra are experiencing as the vibrational energy of the universal heart.

Holographic Spirals

Spirals exist throughout Nature at all scales of existence, from the spirals of DNA within the cells of all biological life to the majesty of spiral galaxies. They are innately creative, for their cycles are dynamic, expansive and open-ended.

The psycho-social spirals described by the SDi model take us from our past to our present level of development and reveal the potential of our future. They describe our social evolution from the family groups of prehistory to the tribes, nations and empires of the last few millennia and the emergent global comm-unity of the present and future.

Our psychological growth is also encompassed by this model. Our individual and collective awareness has expanded from being egocentric to ethno-centric and is now becoming world-centric.

But, as Beck and Cowan emphasize, our human family is comprised of all these levels of awareness *at the same time.*

As we begin to attain the interdependency characterized by our global comm-unity, we need to be aware that this time of transition is truly a crisis offering risk and opportunity. And we need to be aware of further insights offered by the SDi approach to change.

Situations

A further aspect of the spirals of awareness proposed by SDi is that different situational factors and stress levels engender different modes of expression. For instance an individual or a culture can operate on, say, the Orange level with regard to their own perceived community whilst operating on the Red level regarding those they consider foreign. And in times of stress they may revert from the Orange to the Blue level in relation to their own populace.

In the case of the awakening of our own chakras, if the lower psychological levels are imbalanced and not integrated as we move to higher levels of awareness, remaining issues allied to the lower chakras will be reactivated. The SDi research maintains that the same occurs when radical change is imposed on people and groups who are not yet ready to embrace it.

So Beck and Cowan argue that sustainable change can generally only occur in small stages. Thus in their own work they encourage processes of change that respect and meet people where they are at rather than attempt to impose radical transformation, with its inherent risks of failure and regression. As such they offer practical assistance to support people to more evolved paradigms, but no more than half a level ahead at a time.

Across all levels, both individuals and cultures are also described by the SDi approach as being potentially open, arrested or closed to change. When they are open, the choice to move to a higher level of awareness can be offered. This is a strategy that can be transformational. When they are arrested at a particular stage, evolutionary rather than revolutionary strategies are required. But when they are closed, transformation can generally only come about through revolutionary change in environmental circumstances – essentially forcing people to change or perish.

Conditions

The dynamic nature of the SDi model allows us to consider not only the levels of awareness that people and cultures embody and their potential for change, but also the conditions that need to be met if sustainable change is to be attained.

There are six fundamental conditions for sustainable change according to Beck and Cowan. As you read through them, you may wish to consider how they apply not only on communal levels but in your own life, too:

The first we've already discussed: there needs to be openness to the possibility of change.

The second is again a holographic resonance of our personal growth. If there are residual issues existing at a lower level, change at a higher level will be unachievable or expressed in an imbalanced way unless and until those lower level issues are resolved.

There also needs to be dissonance with the circumstances of the current level of awareness, otherwise the opportunity to change will be ignored, denied or disdained.

Fourthly, there needs to be an understanding of the underlying causes of such existing dissonance and an awareness of alternative strategies for its resolution.

Whatever barriers to change exist, they need to be identified and appropriately dealt with.

Finally, with any degree of significant change there will almost inevitably be initial confusion relating to the new way of being. During this period of consolidation, when the new memes are progressively embodied, there needs to be ongoing support and validation for the newly emergent world-view.

The Turning of the Tide

The benefits of the SDi approach are its fluidity, dynamism and inclusion. Its processes are replete with metaphors that describe the fundamental nature of the holographic Cosmos: waves, streams, harmonics and resonance. It also recognizes the interplay between gradual, evolutionary change and quantum leaps in awareness.

Over the years, the theory of evolution has been substantially modified from Darwin's initial proposition and now recognizes that gradualism is punctuated by revolutionary change. Ultimately, it is the interacting complementarities of these forms of change that have, over the last four billion years, accounted for the emergence of the human species.

Our entire racial history has also experienced the juxtaposition of periods of slow evolutionary change and rapid revolutionary leaps. Indeed, it's difficult to discern an example of paradigm shifts that have not been revolutionary in both their speed and associated turmoil.

Whilst the lessons of history and the SDi research have shown us that such shifts are unsustainable when imposed on a fixed mindset, they can and do arise when the time and circumstances are ripe.

The old adage states that 'Time and tide wait for no man.' I believe that we're now at the time of the turning of such a tide.

The 8th Level

Astrological influences not only engender the diversity of our individual personalities but also influence human evolution on generational and collective levels. We saw in Chapter 8 how astrological Ages embody a three-fold influence and we discussed how the emergent Age of Aquarius combines the seeding of the Aquarian energies, the peaking of the energies of the Age of Pisces and the falling away of the energetic Age of Aries. The astrological essence of this emergent Age resonates with the eighth level of the SDi model. Whilst this Turquoise level of awareness is embryonic, astrological indicators strongly suggest that it may achieve critical mass in an exponentially short period of time.

As we as individuals choose to access the newly available energies of the 8th chakra of the universal heart, we become pioneers of such awareness. And we become contributors in the attainment of the critical mass that supports our collective Shift of consciousness.

Compete to Co-operate

One of the key requirements for us on comm-unal levels is to balance competitive behaviour with co-operation. The ethos of competition arises from a perception of the world as inherently comprised of scarce resources. Its fundamental assumption is based on a win-lose equation.

Whilst recognizing that many resources are indeed scarce, co-operation aims to arrive at win-win solutions to situations. But how do we learn to co-operate?

Not everyone realizes that co-operation may be beneficial. On a personal level, we're all likely to have encountered selfish and anti-social behaviour that at least in the short term has garnered material benefit. There are many groups and indeed countries in the world today that still perceive competition and aggression as more beneficial to their interests than co-operation. Yet global challenges may be greater now than at any other time in our history. So how can we learn how to co-operate collectively?

Political scientist Robert Axelrod asked this question in the 1970s. He challenged people who play games for a living to devise the best strategy for co-operation between two players as measured by the benefits derived in terms of mutual trust and harmonious relationships.

A key requisite of the game, however, was the inability of the players to communicate and thus negotiate. Under these conditions, not unusual in human affairs, the strategy that won was called 'Tit for Tat', or TFT for short.

This winning game began by the two players co-operating and its only rule was that after that a player did whatever their opponent had done in the previous round.

Afterwards, Axelrod identified four characteristics of a successful strategy:

- Don't be the first to offend.
- Always reciprocate.
- Respond to the other player rather than second-guess them.
- Do the best you can for yourself and those you represent without trying to outdo the other player.

Reconcile

In the basic game, the assumed lack of communication between the players didn't allow for anything other than the prescriptive tit-for-tat response to an offence. However, if that offence wasn't deliberate, but a mistake, not only did

TFT respond with a further offence but the strategy became locked and both players were unable to escape from the cycle.

When the strategy was modified to allow for human fallibility and allowed some offences to go 'unpunished', however, it offered the opportunity to break free from a cycle of offence and counter-offence.

TFT and other games have shown that tit-for-tat responses are unable to ever get out of a pattern of offending. The multi-generational tragedies of such cycles can still be seen today in the Balkans and the Middle East. Only by being willing to forgive a degree of fallibility by both sides or by being willing to be contrite will the pattern be broken and the opportunity for peace emerge.

Reconciliation, however, requires the intention to do so by both sides. In an atmosphere of mistrust and cynicism, little progress can be made. What is needed is a commitment to honesty, a willingness to move towards forgiveness and the development of a mutual attitude of respect and inclusion.

In South Africa F.W. de Klerk and Nelson Mandela brokered the end of apartheid, with the support of the international community, because both leaders embodied such intention and attitudes.

Justice is key to the reconciliation of any such cycle and to the sustainability of any settlement. To facilitate the process of forgiveness and reconciliation, courts of justice were set up in post-apartheid South Africa to openly acknowledge the abuses of those earlier years, bring to justice the perpetrators and release both individuals and society from their guilt and anger.

South Africa was fortunate in having visionary leaders who were able to see beyond the apparent inevitability of the status quo and were willing to embody the aspirations of their people.

Whilst such leaders may be primary catalysts for transformational change, they are now arising not only from the ranks of political parties around the world. For empowered individuals accessing the energies of the 8th chakra are now discovering their authentic voices and becoming the seed-points of cultural and global change.

Heal the Whole

In earlier chapters we've considered ways in which we may heal on a personal basis and in the last chapter we undertook a 12-step journey to wholeness. The emerging understanding of the holographic Cosmos and the lessons of history both inform us that the journey to our collective healing mirrors that of each of us. As we heal the one, we heal the whole. Every step that we need to take to heal ourselves is a step that needs to be taken somewhere in the world today.

The awareness of the second tier of human development, the Yellow and Turquoise levels, progressively embodies the perception of the holographic Cosmos. The consciousness expressed through the Yellow-level world-view is one that recognizes the innate flow of Nature in all its miraculous abundance. The focus is on flexibility and enrichment of experience without harming others. The interweaving and diversity of expression are valued and the totality of cultures around the world is appreciated. Ancient teachings begin to be reappraised and honoured, the Earth is reconsidered as a living being, sites of sanctity are rediscovered and the wisdom of the heart is re-embraced. There is openness to learning and the acquisition of knowledge on an ongoing basis. Such learning is bespoke to each person; for some it is primarily intellectual, for others experiential. It involves acquiring skills that are both useful and enjoyable. Change is recognized as being inevitable, fears relating to its unknowns recede and surfing its waves is understood as a key requirement for inner growth and contentment. Trying to plan in detail is perceived as being less relevant than making the most aware choices in the present moment.

The awareness embodied by the Yellow world-view is nonetheless primarily self-focused. As the Yellow level transitions to that of Turquoise, a truly global perspective and a more profound sense of comm-unity begin to emerge. The holographic nature of the Cosmos is revealed and its underlying unity is directly perceived. Science and Spirit are reconciled in an expanded world-view and the wholistic understanding of consciousness is sought.

While valuing the uniqueness of every person, this level of awareness aims to harmonize an empowered collective of individuals. It facilitates organizations and institutions that are distributed, flexible and co-creative, and in which a multiplicity of stakeholders actively participate.

Shared Values

We may now suggest what some of the shared values of the Yellow and Turquoise levels of awareness may be. There are eight such values, whose wisdom, I feel, is perennial – as right yesterday as it is today and will be tomorrow. As together we step into the universal heart of the 8th chakra, we are ready to embrace and embody their wisdom in our lives. They are:

- Balance of our rights and responsibilities.
- Balance of our needs and our service to others.
- Equality of opportunity.
- Mutual respect.

- Authenticity and integrity in all our dealings – truth, transparency and justice.
- Inclusivity.
- Compassion in action by treating others as we would wish to be treated.
- Reverence for Gaia and all her children.

These values are especially needed at this momentous time when change is not evolutionary but revolutionary. At the most fundamentally physical level, we need to transform our individual and collective way of life in order to survive.

Comm-unity

The levels of awareness we've been exploring are open-ended and the spiral of our individual and collective consciousness continues to evolve. In the next chapter, we'll discuss how we're now becoming able to comm-une not only as a human family but also with Gaia and the multi-dimensional levels of the Cosmos.

As we awaken to our own higher awareness we are able to see, perhaps for the first time, not only how far we have travelled along the path of apparent separation, but also how to come HoME.

CHAPTER 12

Re-member

For at least the last 5,000 years, geomancers have perceived the holographic nature of the Cosmos and have sought to harmonize Heaven and Earth, people and places, to bring well-being and abundance. Although different traditions have accreted knowledge that has been specific to their own era and culture, they have all adhered to the same underlying cosmic principles and all honoured the world as sacred.

The intuitive insights of those sages are being re-evaluated and expanded by the discoveries of wholistic science. The elements that are perennial and universal are now being recognized as forming the foundations of the emerging paradigm of the holographic Cosmos.

To comprehend the Cosmos and our own place within it, such geomancers have sought knowledge gained by the mind. Shamanic traditions, in contrast, have emphasized the wisdom of the heart, and mystics have embodied the divine will that creates the world. Now, for the first time, we have access to the wisdom teachings and spiritual traditions of our entire human family and we are aware of all three paths to understanding and enlightenment.

In the universal heart of the 8th chakra, we are able to bring together these three approaches that reflect the three fundamental aspects of ourselves – mind, heart and will – to gain a more profound perception of the Cosmos than ever before. As we embody the energies of the 8th and higher transpersonal chakras, we are able to connect directly with the wider Cosmos and higher aspects of ourselves. We are becoming able to commune with Gaia as a living being and to re-establish a profound relationship with her and her multi-dimensional realms.

Learn to Listen

When we meet someone for the first time, the best way for us to get to know them is to listen to what they have to say. Unlike our ancestors and the precious few primary peoples who still walk the Earth, however, most of us have not considered our planetary home, Gaia, as a living being. Whilst we may have appreciated her beauty and abundance, berated her vicissitudes or been awed by her power, our culture has not yet recognized her as being innately alive. If we are to get to know her once more, we should listen to her.

But listen to whom?

As young children, we do often encounter the discarnate realms of Gaia and their many voices. Known by many names – Faeries, Devas, Elementals, Angels – they are natural and familiar to us. That is, until the adults around us deny their existence and convince us to mistrust our own experiences.

As parapsychologists are progressively appreciating, if our ego-mind is closed to anything other than what we term materialistic 'reality', then we are literally unable to see beyond its limitations. Therefore, if we are not open to the possibility of the presence of these beings, we will be unable to 'see' them.

Whilst most people still refuse to acknowledge this possibility, more and more sane and well-grounded people, through their own direct experiences, are reconnecting with these realms.

Devas

The terms we'll use here to describe these different realms are those that may already be familiar to you. Geomancers and other sensitives perceive that elemental beings exist on aetheric levels superimposed upon and able to interact with the physical plane.

The Sanskrit word *Devas*, meaning 'shining ones', is often used to describe the beings who direct and guide natural forces and processes throughout the planetary consciousness that is Gaia.

Whilst the adjective 'devic' is also sometimes used to describe the angelic realms, Angels are generally deemed to be associated with humanity and animals, whereas Devas are usually associated with plants and the elemental world.

From time immemorial, devic beings have consistently been reported as ranging from tiny nature spirits to great landscape guardians. They are associated with the archetypal elements of Earth, Water, Air and Fire and the names respectively given to their related nature spirits are gnomes, undines, sylphs and salamanders. Additionally, there are nature spirits associated with plants and trees that are commonly known as dryads. A number of traditions perceive a seven-fold spiritual hierarchy of such beings, rising from nature spirits to the angelic realms.

My own understanding arises from the direct communication I've enjoyed with Devas and Angels over many years. It is that over aeons of time nature spirits associated with a single archetypal element are able to evolve into those who combine two, three or four elements. It is these who become the beings we call Devas and who are associated with the spiritual and physical stewardship of places and landscapes. They too are able to evolve further into the beings we know as Angels.

Communing

In my own experience and in working with thousands of people around the world, I've discovered some simple principles for communing with such beings that we'll now discuss.

To begin with, I must stress that for each of us, our connections with these realms are expressed in different ways. For some of us, our inner vision offers us an insight – or inner-sight – into their realities. Others may feel or sense their presence. Yet others may hear their voices on an inner plane. No way is right and no way is wrong – each is just our way.

Whatever your own intuitive experiencing naturally is, I would encourage you to use it fully, rather than attempt to develop a different way – just as if you were a natural virtuoso on the piano, I'd suggest you practise to improve your gift rather than turning your attention to, say, learning the violin. As you continue to explore, however, you may discover that your innate way of perceiving naturally develops to include other means as well. If that happens, let it evolve naturally, rather than trying to force it.

One other important point is that whereas on the physical plane appearances are generally fairly fixed, on the mental and higher planes that nature spirits inhabit, it seems that they are able to change their appearance at will. They can display themselves in forms that either reflect our own cultural bias or that best conveys their message to us.

Angels

With intention supported by practice and experience, we can directly connect with all the devic and angelic realms of Gaia.

We can do this wherever we are. Whilst the countryside is a wonderful place to experience the incredible beauty of Nature, we can commune with the devic and angelic realms anywhere and at any time. The attunement on page 251 is offered to help you be in the energetic vibrations of the 8th chakra and the 9th or earthstar chakra and thus to facilitate your connection with these realms of Gaia.

The most important requirements for such connections are willingness and openness. As with all good relationships, there also needs to be mutual respect, honesty, love and gratitude. The devic and angelic realms embody these and so must you if your relationships with these beings are to thrive and guide your inner growth.

In recent years many books have been written on how to communicate with the angelic realms and there are four Archangels, Uriel, Gabriel, Raphael and Michael, whose guidance and influence is paramount. Each takes spiritual responsibility and guardianship for the expression of one of the archetypal elements on a planetary basis and Michael is also deemed by many to be the spiritual guide leading and supporting the Shift of human and planetary consciousness at this time. As such he is a marvellous mentor for our communion with all the angelic and devic realms, and asking for his ongoing guidance safely and generously supports our exploration and communion with the realms of Gaia.

When we need inspiration and the Fire of creativity and truth to flow through us, Michael will also help us.

When we need to ground an intention or an outcome, or our inner query or issue relates to the element of Earth, then we may also ask for the aid of Uriel.

Where we require greater clarity of thought or our quest involves the element of Air, we may seek the support of Raphael.

And when we feel the need for healing, either of others or ourselves, or we are connecting to the element of Water, we may call on Gabriel for strength and support.

Healing Rifts

Throughout *The 8th Chakra* we've undertaken a journey of healing. And just as there are energetic rifts to heal within us and within our human family, so there are rifts throughout the Earth where we have been responsible for pollution and destruction. There are also very many places where the historical imprints of human traumas have left energetic scars. The residual energies of these continue to affect us by holding us in outworn patterns of behaviour. Their healing is now important to enable ever-more people to liberate themselves from the energetic imprisonment of the past.

The holographic and conscious nature of the Cosmos reveals that our outer environment reflects our inner state. We need to acknowledge this inherent resonance in recognizing such environmental imbalances and, with the help of the angelic and devic realms, seeking to understand and resolve them.

In Chapter 7, we saw how the energetic meridians of Gaia can become blocked. Whilst not generally harmful to the Earth herself, these imbalanced energies can resonate with us in ways that are harmful to us. So let's now consider how to diagnose and heal such geopathic stress with the higher guidance of the angelic and devic realms.

Geopathic Stress

Our consciousness is expressed energetically through the coherence and interactions of electromagnetic fields. Imbalances in such EM fields within the environment are the main mechanism of geopathic stress.

Just over a century ago our understanding of such fields was rudimentary and yet now we have become almost wholly reliant on technologies that utilize their principles. Our environment is now suffused with the artificially produced energetic waveforms of such fields to an extent unthinkable even a few decades ago.

Evidence continues to accumulate that being continually close to high-level EM fields such as those of overhead power lines and mobile phones adversely affects our health. These are issues which geomancers have appreciated for some time.

The high number of electrical appliances in offices and homes almost certainly contributes to ill health, especially when their effects are combined in people who are already energetically stressed by other factors. Indeed, such lifestyle-related stress may be a crucial factor in reducing our natural immune system to levels that are below the threshold for our body to naturally attune itself to these new energetic circumstances.

Energetic Imprints

Energetic disruptions are not only caused by geopathic stress. Whilst fewer of us are living in older homes, newer houses are now very often built on land that has previously been built on. Our built environment is thus pervaded by the energetic imprints of the past.

Such residual energies range from the merely stagnant to

those that carry the imprint of previous traumas such as battles. They may also be associated with a variety of sentient entities. Negative thought-forms and emotionally-charged spirit presences may be attached to a building or associated with the land on which it is built. Given the multi-dimensionality of the Cosmos, there are also places that are essentially inter-dimensional connecting-points.

In attuning and asking the angelic realms, especially Michael, for guidance on the causes of geopathic stress, if you become aware that any energetic disruption may be caused by a historical imprint or a sentient being, unless you gain clear guidance that you are able to deal with the problem yourself and should appropriately do so, please call in someone with greater understanding and experience to help. Whilst there is an open invitation by the angelic and devic realms for those who choose to empower themselves in accessing their guidance, there is no place for ego-based me-powerment at these levels.

Geomantic Design

The *feng shui* practitioners of ancient China and the *vaastu* sages of India have known the energetic principles of geomantic design for millennia. Their traditions and the less well-known understanding of the ancient geomancers of Europe are now being recognized by our collective awareness.

All such traditions aim to optimize the flow of life-promoting energies through the location, orientation, shape and layout of buildings themselves and their relationship to their surrounding landscape. The timing of events relating to a building is also traditionally taken into account in order to optimize the prevailing astrological influences.

Understanding and resolving serious or complex energetic

problems generally takes years of experience and so a professional practitioner usually best deals with the resolution of issues relating to such serious imbalances and sentient presences. However, by understanding the principles we've explored in *The 8th Chakra* and by attuning to our own higher guidance and that of the angelic and devic realms, we can become intuitively aware of how to optimally balance the energies and clear the space of our own homes.

Space Clearing

In this work, simplicity and a positive and loving intention are the keys to success. Also, we may consider where we are as merely a place to live or we can consider it to be our home. So before you begin, set the intention that however you've previously felt about the place in which you live, this gift of

Your first step in space clearing your home is to ensure that it is clean, tidy and uncluttered. If it's dirty, untidy or filled with 'stuff', its energies will inevitably become stagnant. Old clothes, photographs, books or any collections that no longer mean much to you or that you don't use are very good candidates for decluttering. And don't forget to consider the outside condition of your property, your garden and the entrance.

The second and third steps are to attune through the attunement on page 243 to ask both your own higher guidance and Archangel Michael to help determine what imbalances may be present in your home and then what to do to resolve them.

If at this stage you discern imbalanced energies that are beyond your experience or expertise to resolve, please call in professional help. But be assured that this is the case only for a small minority of homes.

Whilst your guidance may involve your doing something physically to balance the energies, and there are a number of books that offer traditional suggestions, more often than not you may be able to resolve any imbalance solely on energetic levels. You may be guided, for example, to work with Michael or one of the other Archangels to cleanse the space by visualizing an energetic shower of rainbow light cascading through it, sensing the fragrance of aetheric flowers or placing a pyramid of golden light over the entire property.

The final aspect of your space clearing is to undertake a simple ceremony of your own choice to thank the Angels and Devas for their guidance and to ask, with gratitude, for a blessing on your home and on all those who live and visit there. This ceremony can be as simple as lighting a candle and saying your words of loving thanks. Just allow yourself to be intuitively guided as to what feels right for you.

space clearing is for both you and your *home*.

When you decide to leave a home, a final space clearing is very helpful. It enables you to move on freely and be open to the new possibilities in your life and it allows your property to welcome someone new. I've known many people who've tried to sell a property without success until it's been space cleared.

Undertaking a space clearing when you arrive at somewhere new also clears the space of the imprint of previous owners or tenants and enables you to establish a loving and caring relationship with your new home from the beginning.

If at any point during your space clearing you are unsure of your intuitive guidance, you may wish to consider dowsing as either an alternative means of attunement or as a method of validation.

Dowsing

The ancient art of dowsing, where nonlocal awareness is utilized to discover things that are beyond the five physical senses has, over the last few years, enjoyed a resurgence. Whilst dowsing for water, or water divining, is the best-known and most common use of dowsing skills, practitioners can attune themselves to dowse for virtually anything.

Dowsing may also be used as a means of diagnosis, for decision-making, for health, as a means of accessing and validating our own higher guidance and for space clearing.

The process involves our energetic attunement to whatever we're seeking to find. It is similar to tuning a wireless or television to the wavelength of a particular station. In the case of dowsing, we are the wireless and what we're attuning to takes the place of the wireless station.

Such attunement is essentially the same as the nonlocal awareness achieved by remote viewers. As is the case for such 'at a distance' perception, our bodies may pick up more subliminal information than our conscious minds. It is the minute muscle reactions of our bodies that the 'tools' of the dowser then magnify. So, whilst the usual tools are either pendulums or hand-held bent rods of wood or metal, the tool itself is merely a means of registering the attuned response. Any tool – or indeed nothing – can be used if it works for the individual.

We can all dowse. And practice will increase our abilities. Also, dowsing, like meditation, by requiring us to be centred and still, enables us to attune not only to our own quiet voice of inner wisdom but also to the voice of Gaia and the wisdom of the Cosmos.

Once you've chosen your preferred dowsing tool, in order to begin to dowse you need to feel calm and balanced physically, emotionally and mentally. If you are feeling anxious, you can calm yourself by taking a few deep breaths.

The next step is to elicit a yes/positive and no/negative response from your pendulum or rods. Quiet your mind and ask on an inner level to be shown first a 'yes' and then a 'no'. If you are using a pendulum, the usual response is for it to swing clockwise or counter-clockwise. If you are working with rods, these should be free to swing to the right or left. The pendulum or rods should swing one way for 'yes' and the other way for 'no'. Repeat this step every time you undertake a session of dowsing, for you may find that the direction of the 'yes/no' responses sometimes flips between sessions!

Calm and Balanced

Practise by first checking the dowsing response to questions you already know the answers to and then by seeking answers to questions you don't know the answers to but can independently validate. Keep at it until your confidence increases. Once you are able to trust your dowsing, you can then move on to asking questions where dowsing may be the primary or only means of obtaining an answer.

Also learn to ask clearly defined questions that can only elicit a 'yes/no' response. Sometimes your dowsing tools may not respond. In this case consider rephrasing the question.

If you are seeking answers to questions that involve others or issues that are contentious, your first questions should be to confirm that it's appropriate for you to dowse for these reasons at this time.

If you are dowsing for something in particular, many dowsers use what are called 'witnesses' to help them to tune into the target. Witnesses are usually small enough to fit into the palm of your hand or be carried easily in a pocket, for example a small bottle of water, if water is what you are attempting to locate.

When determining the possibility of geopathic stress in your home, you can dowse for answers for its presence, location, type (e.g. water, electromagnetism) and strength. By drawing a plan of your home on paper, you can also pendulum dowse to trace any lines of stress on the plan.

To further develop your dowsing skills, the dowsing societies in a number of countries, including Britain, the U.S., Canada and Australia, run courses for beginners through to advanced students.

Finally, if you are dowsing on a personal level and feel that your rational mind can get in the way, you may try blind dowsing by using a pendulum. Here you write on a number of pieces of paper the range of answers to a particular question. Then you fold and shuffle the papers in such a way that you can't differentiate between them. Lay each out on a flat surface and hold the pendulum over each piece of paper in turn, while asking if this is the answer that is for your highest good.

The more you practise your inherent dowsing skills, the greater your energetic sensitivity and conscious resonance will become. And so will your ability to hear the wisdom of Gaia.

Gaia's Shifting, Too

Gaia is also readying herself for a Shift of consciousness and as we connect with her awareness through the energetic portals of the 8th and ninth chakras we can consciously aid her (and ourselves) through this process.

Geomancers are noting this energetic Shift of Gaia in a number of significant ways in addition to the physical shifts of her climate and surface features. The first is that the energy meridians that have previously been perceived as embodying polarity energies are now being seen as embodying a three-fold interweaving of positive/male, negative/female and neutral/child. These triadic energies are the equivalent of our mind, heart and will, and their activation reflects our own activation of the 8th chakra of the universal heart.

In Chapter 7, we discussed the 12-fold Unity grid of Gaia. Embodying the ever-present 'memory' of unity awareness, it is also awakening at this time in the same way as we are now able to access the higher chakras of our 12-fold transpersonal awareness. Its ongoing activation is told in my forthcoming book *The 13th Step*. When completely activated it too will embody the 13th transformational wholeness of unity awareness – and *is* the Shift in consciousness that is being prophesied.

Geomancer Richard Leviton has termed the geomantic consciousness of this 12-fold activation of Gaia an Albion. In ancient times, this was the mystic name of Britain. Visionary William Blake used the term to describe the cosmic human being – our original state and our future destiny.

Albions are the devic equivalent of the soular hero and such planetary consciousness is activated through human, devic and angelic co-operation. As an Albion fully awakens, it embodies the cosmic template of unity consciousness.

At its wholly activated level the dodecahedral Unity grid is a planetary Albion. Holographically, all the 12 pentagonal divisions of the Unity grid are also Albions in their fully activated states and so on at ever-smaller scales throughout the landscapes of Gaia.

Our Soular System, Too

The group soul that is our Soular System has been guided

from its inception by cosmic beings known in some traditions as the Elohim. Their role as mentors and watchers over the evolution of consciousness within our Soular System is explored further in *The 13th Step*.

As we are beginning to access the transpersonal perception of our tenth chakra, we are becoming able to connect consciously with the Elohim and the planetary beings of our Soular System. Whilst astrologers have perceived their profound influence for millennia, we are only now realizing that they are archetypal aspects of our soular consciousness. With this expanded awareness, we can now commune with the Sun, Moon and planets in ways that enable us to understand ourselves and each other at a more profound level than ever before.

Over the portal of the ancient oracle at Delphi, Greece, was the injunction 'Know thyself.' As we connect with the archetypal consciousness of our Soular System, we can now truly know who we are.

In doing so, as with our communion with the realms of Gaia, we will begin not only to be aware of the vastness of the Cosmos, but also to recognize our true spiritual place in its co-creation.

Galactic Awareness

As we walk – and dance – together towards the culmination of aeons and the Shift of consciousness of the year 2012/2013, cosmic forces support and illuminate our path.

In early November 2003 an astrological alignment comprising the Sun, Moon, Mars, Jupiter, Saturn and Chiron formed a perfect six-pointed star in the sky. The resonance of this unique cosmic mandala, known globally as the Harmonic Concordance, with the emergent energies of the 8th and higher chakras supported each one of us to walk the journey of the soular hero.

Forty-four days after the Harmonic Concordance was the December solstice of 2003. This 23rd day of the 12th month of that year added up to and embodied the numerology of 13 (23 being 2 + 3 = 5, the 12th month being 1 + 2 = 3 and 2003 being 2 + 3 = 5, adding up 5 + 3 + 5 = 13). This shortest day of the year in the northern hemisphere completed the three-day period of the winter solstice, when the rising Sun 'stands still' – the time of the rebirth of the solar/soular hero. And the Druids of ancient Britain, whose lunar calendar of 13 months of 28 days each totalled 364 days, considered this day which reconciled the lunar and solar year as being 'out of time'.

This was also the exact day and year when, after 26,000 years, the Sun was aligned with Ophiucus, the 13th zodiac sign and thus the center of the galaxy.

This moment was the culmination of my own higher guidance, which had led my fellow travellers and me on an extraordinary inner and outer journey around the world. Now as we stood together in the great stone circle at Avebury, England, which geomancers consider to be the planetary umbilical cord with the galactic centre, we lived out what I had been guided by the Elohim to do many years before – to connect with galactic consciousness to open a portal of such higher awareness on a planetary level.

As we continue to journey together in these coming years, the energetic waves of succeeding planetary alignments of our Soular System are acting as cosmic way-showers for our collective leap in awareness. We have almost unimaginable cosmic support at this time as the angelic and devic realms join with the pantheon of Ascended Masters to guide and facilitate our path. With their love and inspiration, at the cusp of the 12th and 13th year of this new millennium, will we be able to take the 12th step of the journey of the soular hero and embody unity consciousness for ourselves and thus for us all?

I don't know. For my own continuing journey is one of discovery as well.

I only know that each of us can make the choice to try.

And that is good enough.

Chapter 13

HoME

We have all chosen, at the level of our higher consciousness, to be here at this time. We have all undertaken a journey of aeons to arrive at this point, but it's time to set down the baggage we have accumulated and be free.

We are the ones we have been waiting for and here and now is our opportunity to be the master navigators of our own consciousness. We can be the co-creators of our future destiny, in alignment and harmony with the flow of the Cosmos.

We are not alone. As we expand our awareness to the transpersonal levels that are now available to us, not only can we choose to undertake the journey of the soular hero but we can also perceive that just as the soular heroes of myth and legend had companions who helped them to fulfil their mission, so we too have support and guidance. We are now able to connect directly with the archetypal aspects of our individual and collective awareness – spiritual guides including the assembly of Angels and the Ascended Masters of all spiritual traditions.

Together we have arrived at this threshold of transformation. The choices we make, individually and collectively, in the next few years will determine not only our destiny but also that of all future generations.

The Chinese sage Lao Tzu once said, 'The journey of 1,000 miles begins with a single step.' In every moment, every breath, every step, we can choose something different from the one before.

If then we chose fear, we can now choose love.

If then we chose tears, we can now choose laughter.

If then we chose death, we can now choose life.

In every moment we co-create the universe afresh. And each and every one of us can make a difference, no matter how small we may feel we are. For, as Anita Roddick once said, 'If you think you're too small to be effective, you've never been in bed with a mosquito.'

Dancing together towards 2012/2013, we can each awaken the 8th chakra of the universal heart within us and undertake the journey of the soular hero. In doing so, we empower others and ourselves, in service to all our relations and in the fulfilment of our collective and cosmic destiny.

As we progressively awaken from our spiritual amnesia and re-member the wholeness of who we *really* are, we are now able to come HoME as together we are able to bring to birth the reality of Heaven on Mother Earth.

> In the universal heart, I re-member
> the wholeness of myself.
> In the universal heart, I re-member
> the wholeness of our human family.
> In the universal heart, I re-member
> the wholeness of Gaia and all her children.
> In the universal heart, I re-member
> the wholeness of our Soular System.
> In the universal heart, I re-member
> the wholeness of our galaxy.

In the universal heart, I re-member
the wholeness of the Cosmos.
As I re-member the wholeness of my soul,
I do so with love, joy and gratitude
in the unity of the One.

Attunement 1

Breath Exercises

Breath *is* life. And the connection between our breath, our thoughts and our emotions is profound. Yet our generally shallow breathing only utilizes about 10 per cent of our lung capacity and results in tiredness and stress. As we breathe more deeply, we literally live life more fully and enhance our general well-being.

Here are three simple breathing exercises.

This first exercise can be done any time and anywhere.

- Stop for a moment. If possible, close your eyes to aid your focus.

- Focusing on your breath, take three breaths.

- For each breath:

  Breathe in slowly through your nose and as you do so, say to yourself, 'I am...'

  Breathe out through your nose equally slowly and as you do so, add the name of whatever energy or essence you choose to embody within yourself at this time, for example, 'Calm, Peace, Loving Truth, Courage, Clarity, Love.'

For the next two exercises, it is easiest to sit on an upright chair with your head, neck and back in alignment and your lower back supported by the chair. Close your eyes to help attain inner focus.

This exercise is useful to balance yourself before undertaking a meditation.

- Place one hand on your abdomen.

- Inhale slowly through your nose, feeling the air fill and expand your abdomen.

- Continue slowly inhaling as you then expand your chest and gently raise your shoulders towards your ears.

- Exhale slowly through your *mouth*, while relaxing first your shoulders and then your chest and finally contracting your abdomen.

- Repeat until you feel balanced and at peace.

This third exercise is useful to identify areas in your body which may be imbalanced and to send them healing.

- Inhale slowly through your nose, hold your breath for a moment and then exhale through your nose equally slowly.

- Breathe in this gentle way for a minute or so until you are able to sense the rising and falling of energy within yourself.

- When you do, allow your attention to follow your breath for a further minute or so and sense if there are any areas of your body where the energy feels stagnant or stuck.

- If there are, visualize (sense, or just intend) that as your breath flows through you it reaches this area and its energy gently dissolves the blockage.

- As you exhale, visualize that the stuck energy is being exhaled too.

- Continue for a further minute or so until you sense the energy of your breath freely flowing through you.

Attunement 2

Personal Chakra Meditation

- First, find a quiet and comfortable place and settle down, preferably sitting upright with your back supported and both feet on the ground.

- Begin with the breath-balancing exercise of Attunement 1.

- When you feel ready, with each in-breath, visualize or sense a beam of white-gold light entering your body through your crown chakra, and as you breathe out, sense the beam of light continuing down your spine and on into the Earth.

- With each breath, sense that any imbalanced or heavy energies are breathed out through your root chakra and released with gratitude into the Earth.

- Now breathe the white-gold light only to the base of your spine as you begin to meditate with the energies of each chakra in turn, beginning with the root chakra.

- At your root chakra, visualize or sense the white-gold light transmuting to a deep ruby red. Between your in- and out-breaths, focus on your bodily senses and feel yourself become physically empowered. As you breathe out, sense yourself radiating the essence of the ruby light and embodying courageous energy.

- Next, at your sacral chakra, envisage the white-gold light becoming a vibrant orange and, between in- and out-breaths, feel yourself embodying vitality and vigour. As you breathe out, radiate the orange light of your joyous energy.

- At your solar plexus chakra, visualize or sense the white-gold light becoming a brilliant golden colour. Between in- and out-breaths, sense your creativity and the expression of your highest purpose. As you breathe out, radiate this golden light.

- At your heart chakra, envisage the white-gold light becoming a sumptuous green and sense the beauty of the loving and compassionate being that you are. Radiate this love as you real-ize that you can choose love in every moment in thought, word and deed.

- At your throat chakra, visualize the white-gold light becoming a vivid sky-blue and allow the authentic expression of your unique creativity to flow as you radiate your loving truth with each out-breath.

- At your third eye chakra, envisage the white-gold light becoming a rich indigo and sense your profound inner wisdom and knowing that all life is One. Feel this spiritual awareness radiate as you breathe out.

- At your crown chakra, visualize the white-gold light flowing up from the base of your spine through each chakra in turn. As it rises to your crown, sense it becoming an exquisite violet glow and as you breathe in, fill yourself with this beautiful light.

- Finally, as you breathe out, radiate the energy of your divine self to the Cosmos, sharing love, joy and gratitude with all beings.

Attunement 3

Universal Heart and Earthstar Chakra Meditation

- First, find a quiet and comfortable place and settle down, preferably sitting upright with your back supported and both feet on the ground.

- Begin by taking a few deep breaths. With each in-breath, envisage that you are breathing in the essence of a peaceful joy and allow it to flow through and fill your entire body. With each out-breath, allow any distraction or concern to be gently released without effort. Continue to breathe in this way until you feel balanced and at ease.

- Now focus your attention in the area of your heart chakra and breathe into the essence of its loving energy. As you do so, sense a sphere of light beginning to form here. You may visualize this or just sense its energy.

- Continue to breathe into the sphere of light and with each breath envisage or sense the sphere expanding and its energy becoming brighter as it grows to the size that you intuitively know is perfect for you at this time. As it expands to become its perfect size, feel its essence of loving compassion and feel yourself loved and nurtured for *all* that you are, without condition or judgement.

- Now envisage or sense the sphere of heart energy gently moving up through your body, coming to rest at the alter major chakra at the base of your skull, where your skull meets the top of your backbone. As the heart chakra resonates with the essence of love, so the alter major chakra resonates with the essence of mind.

- Now sense a second sphere of light begin to form here, within the sphere of heart energy. Again you may envisage it or just feel its presence.

- With each breath, sense it growing in size and brightness and feel its essence of clarity and intuitive wisdom.

- Envisage or sense it continuing to expand until it becomes the same size as the heart sphere. Now sense the two spheres of heart and mind energy nested within each other gently merging together to form a single sphere of heart and mind essence, their energies balancing and becoming whole.

- Now sense the combined sphere of energy moving down through your body to come to rest at your solar plexus chakra and connect with the energies of your will and intention.

- Begin to focus on your breath flowing into your solar plexus chakra and envisage a third sphere of light forming here within the sphere of heart-mind essence and again growing with each breath in size and brightness. Sense its essence of highest intention and purpose as it expands to become the same size as the sphere of heart-mind energy and then envisage the spheres merging to form one.

- Finally, sense the combined sphere of heart-mind-will energy moving easily and gently up through your body until coming to rest midway between your heart and throat chakras. This is the energetic centre of the 8th or universal heart chakra, the portal to the transpersonal chakras of your unity chakra energy field.

- Envisage this portal opening as you breathe into the universal heart of the 8th chakra. Now sense a pulse of energy reaching up from your 8th chakra to connect you with your highest awareness, purpose and guidance.

- Sense a returning pulse of energy flowing through the 8th chakra down through your body to a point about six inches below your feet. This is the 9th, earthstar, chakra, which you may visualize or sense as a vortex of energy. From here, pulse the energy deep into the heart of the Earth and sense a returning pulse of energy from the heart of Gaia up and through your earthstar chakra and into the 8th chakra.

- Continue in harmony with your breath to pulse a column of energy connecting your 8th chakra with

your highest awareness and then down through the
earthstar to connect with the awareness of Gaia until
you feel balanced and well grounded.

- At this point, as you feel appropriate, breathe into the
universal heart and call upon your highest guidance
for re-membering and healing into the wholeness of
who you *really* are.

- When you feel ready to complete the meditation,
withdraw your awareness and energy back into your
body, offer thanks to your highest guidance and any
spiritual guides that you may work with, and gently
come back into the room.

As discussed in Chapter 9, you may work with this
meditation to receive your own highest guidance relating to
the healing of yourself and others, to release any limiting
fears that you embody and to perceive and ground your
higher purpose and way forward.

Further Reading

Don Beck and Christopher Cowan, *Spiral Dynamics: Mastering values, leadership and change*, Blackwell Publishing, 2006

Lyn Birkbeck, *Divine Astrology: Enlisting the aid of the planetary powers*, O Books, 2005

Jude Currivan, *The Wave: A life-changing journey into the heart and mind of the Cosmos*, O Books, 2005

James D'Angelo, *The Healing Power of the Human Voice*, Healing Arts Press, 2005

Masaru Emoto, *The Hidden Messages in Water*, Beyond Words Publishing, 2004

Ervin Laszlo, *Science and the Re-enchantment of the Cosmos: The rise of the integral vision of reality*, Inner Traditions, 2006

Bruce Lipton, *The Biology of Belief*, Mountain of Love Publishing, 2005

James Lovelock, *The Revenge of Gaia: Why the Earth is fighting back – and how we can still save humanity*, Allen Lane, 2006

Caroline Myss, *Invisible Acts of Power: Personal choices that create miracles*, Simon & Schuster, 2005

Dean Radin, *Entangled Minds: Extrasensory experiences in a quantum reality*, HarperCollins, 2006

David Tame, *The Secret Power of Music*, Destiny Books, 1984

Eckhart Tolle, *The Power of Now*, Hodder & Stoughton, 1999

Desmond Tutu, *No Future without Forgiveness*, Doubleday, 2000

Websites

College of Psychic Studies: www.collegeofpsychicstudies.co.uk

HeartMath Institute: www.heartmath.com

Monroe Institute – metamusic tapes and CDs: www.newmind.com

Dr Alfred Tomatis – acoustic healing work: www.tomatis.com

Index

About the Author

Jude Currivan is a healer and scientist who has studied consciousness and perennial-wisdom teachings since childhood. She has a master's degree in physics, specializing in cosmology and quantum theory; and a Ph.D. in archaeology, researching ancient cosmologies. Jude is a sensitive who has directly experienced multidimensional realities and worked with higher guidance all her life. Moving on from a highly successful international business career in the mid-1990s, she now travels and teaches worldwide, bringing her lifelong experience and understanding as a healer and cosmic geomancer to facilitate wholeness on personal and collective levels. Her first book, *The Wave,* was published in November 2005.

Details of Jude's international workshop schedule and her healing and cosmic geomantic work are shown on her Website: **www.judecurrivan.com**.

We hope you enjoyed this Hay House book. If you'd like to receive our online catalog featuring additional information on Hay House books and products, or if you'd like to find out more about the Hay Foundation, please contact:

Hay House, Inc., P.O. Box 5100, Carlsbad, CA 92018-5100
(760) 431-7695 or (800) 654-5126
(760) 431-6948 (fax) or (800) 650-5115 (fax)
www.hayhouse.com® • www.hayfoundation.org

———

Published in Australia by: Hay House Australia Pty. Ltd.,
18/36 Ralph St., Alexandria NSW 2015
Phone: 612-9669-4299 • *Fax:* 612-9669-4144
www.hayhouse.com.au

Published in the United Kingdom by: Hay House UK, Ltd.,
The Sixth Floor, Watson House, 54 Baker Street, London W1U 7BU
Phone: +44 (0)20 3927 7290 • *Fax:* +44 (0)20 3927 7291
www.hayhouse.co.uk

Published in India by: Hay House Publishers India,
Muskaan Complex, Plot No. 3, B-2, Vasant Kunj, New Delhi 110 070
Phone: 91-11-4176-1620 • *Fax:* 91-11-4176-1630
www.hayhouse.co.in

———

Access New Knowledge.
Anytime. Anywhere.

Learn and evolve at your own pace
with the world's leading experts.

www.hayhouseU.com

Printed in the United States
By Bookmasters